THE PEOPLE OF NEW FRANCE

This book surveys the social history of New France. For more than a century, until the British conquest of 1759–60, France held sway over a major portion of the North American continent. In this vast territory several unique colonial societies emerged, societies which in many respects mirrored *ancien regime* France, but also incorporated a major Aboriginal component.

Whereas earlier works in this field represented pre-Conquest Canada as entirely white and Catholic, *The People of New France* looks closely at other members of the society as well, including black slaves, English captives, and the Christian Iroquois of the mission villages near Montreal. The artisans, soldiers, merchants, nobles, and priests who congregated in the towns of Montreal and Quebec are the subject of one chapter. Another examines the special situation of French-regime women living under a legal system that recognized wives as equal owners of all family property. The author extends his analysis to French settlements around the Great Lakes and down the Mississippi Valley, and to Acadia and Île Royale.

Greer's book, addressed to undergraduate students and general readers, provides a deeper understanding of how people lived their lives in New France.

ALLAN GREER is a professor in the Department of History at the University of Toronto. He is the author of *The Patriots and the People: The Rebellion of 1837 in Rural Lower Canada* and *Peasant, Lord, and Merchant: Rural Society in Three Quebec Parishes* and the co-editor of *Colonial Leviathan: State Formation in Mid-Nineteenth-Century Canada*. His work has won several awards, including the Prix Lionel-Groulx, the John Porter Award, and the John A. Macdonald Prize.

THEMES IN CANADIAN SOCIAL HISTORY

Editors: Craig Heron and Franca Iacovetta

ALLAN GREER

The People of New France

UNIVERSITY OF TORONTO PRESS
Toronto   Buffalo   London

© University of Toronto Press Incorporated 1997
Toronto Buffalo London

Printed in Canada

ISBN 0-8020-0826-7 (cloth)
ISBN 0-8020-7816-8 (paper)

Printed on acid-free paper

Canadian Cataloguing in Publication Data

Greer, Allan
  The people of New France

  (Themes in Canadian Social History)
  Includes bibliographical references and index.
  ISBN 0-8020-0826-7 (bound)   ISBN 0-8020-7816-8 (pbk.)

  1. Canada – Social conditions – To 1763. 2. Canada –
  Social life and customs – To 1763.* I. Title. II. Series.

  FC350.G73 1997   971.01'8   C97-930994-8
  F1030.G73 1997

University of Toronto Press acknowledges the financial assistance to its publishing program of the Canada Council for the
Arts and the Ontario Arts Council.

TO LOUISE DECHÊNE

Contents

Acknowledgments

Many people helped bring this book to fruition and I would like briefly to record my sincere thanks to them all. Gwen Schulman gathered materials on the trial of the slave Angélique, and Carolyn Podruchny prepared the map and the index. Louise Dechêne, Brenda Gainer, Ralph Greer, Jan Noel, and Tom Wien provided critical readings of the text, which saved me from numerous errors of style and content. I also benefited from the thoughtful and thorough critiques of my students in History 362 at the University of Toronto. Thanks are due also to copy-editor Beverley Beetham Endersby. Demanding and rigorous, yet unfailingly encouraging, series editor Craig Heron managed to strike just the right balance. His situation as a historian specializing in other fields and different centuries provided the ideal 'outsider's perspective' needed to fine-tune an introductory text dealing with the French regime. Though less closely involved with the book than Craig, series co-editor Franca Iacovetta and Gerry Hallowell of University of Toronto Press also provided valuable feedback and generally smoothed the path.

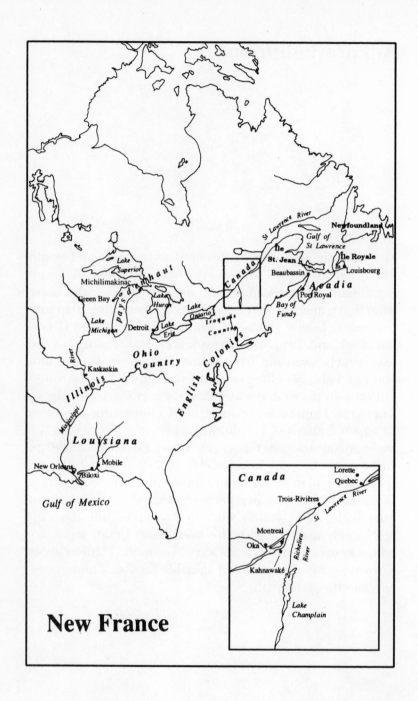

New France

THE PEOPLE OF NEW FRANCE

Introduction

When Europeans intruded into eastern North America in the seventeenth century, France was a leading player. Brought to the shores of the continent by the bounty of the Atlantic cod fishery, drawn into the gaping mouth of the St Lawrence by the lure of the fur trade, the French eventually established year-round settlements in Acadia (modern Nova Scotia) and 'Canada' (now the province of Quebec). Later, after 1700, additional colonies were founded: Louisiana, on the Gulf of Mexico; Illinois, up the Mississippi; Detroit, on Lake Erie; and Île Royale, far to the east, on Cape Breton Island. Linking these small enclaves of European settlement were vast territories occupied by aboriginal nations but claimed by France with the arrogant presumptuousness of the imperialist. Certainly there was a genuine French presence extending through the Mississippi valley and the Great Lakes region, but it consisted of communications links, commercial networks, and Native alliances and was not based on fully developed colonial rule. When people spoke three centuries ago of 'la Nouvelle-France,' they often had in mind this far-flung collection of European settlements, frontier outposts, spheres of influence, and territorial pretensions which constituted the French North American empire. That was 'New France,' in the broad sense of the term.

'New France' was frequently used in a much narrower sense, as a synonym for 'Canada.' The area comprising

Quebec City, Montreal, and the intervening farming districts that edged the St Lawrence River was by far the most intensively colonized portion of French North America. Canada was the political and military headquarters for the wider New France, and it was home to about 90 per cent of the empire's European population; no wonder contemporaries tended to equate this one colonial enclave with New France itself.

Shamelessly exploiting the ambiguity built into the geographic vocabulary of an earlier age, this book on the people of New France tries to have it both ways. Through most of this volume, the focus is on the colonial society of Canada, but one final chapter provides an overview of that more extensive New France which lay to the east and to the southwest of France's premier North American settlement.

As did most colonial peoples in the Americas, the French population of Canada grew and flourished in the graveyards of the original inhabitants. We know that the banks of the St Lawrence were thickly lined with Iroquoian villages when Jacques Cartier visited the area in the 1530s, but by the early seventeenth century this entire people had disappeared, leaving a thinly occupied territory frequented by small bands of nomadic Montagnais and Algonquins. What had happened to the St Lawrence Iroquois? Had they been wiped out by epidemic diseases? Were they destroyed in war? Or did they simply move away? Whatever the precise mechanism of depopulation, it seems clear that it stemmed ultimately from the disrupting intrusions of European traders and explorers. In addition to Cartier's officially sanctioned expeditions, there were innumerable visits by fishermen and whalers throughout the sixteenth century; towards the end of the century, French ships were anchoring in the St Lawrence every year with the express purpose of purchasing furs from the inhabitants. Inadvertently, no doubt, these sixteenth-century visitors created a space in which later French newcomers could gain a toe-hold, settle permanently, and gradually transform the river valley into a predominantly European environment, complete with Old World plants, animals, and, in ever-increasing numbers, people.

It was in 1608, just about the time that the English and the Dutch were establishing colonies elsewhere on the continent, that Quebec was planted as a year-round settlement and the French began to take root. The Montagnais and Algonquins who hunted here in the early 1600s welcomed the newcomers as allies and trading partners. Numbering only a handful at first, the French moved into this devastated landscape, not as conquering invaders, but as a new tribe negotiating a place for itself in the diplomatic webs of Native North America. They were soon linked to most of the northern nations, though this alliance entailed conflict with their friends' enemies, the Five Nations of the Iroquois League, who resided south of Lake Ontario.

For a long time, French immigration to the Canadian colony remained a meagre trickle. Much more isolated from Europe than were Virginia, Massachusetts, or New Netherlands, New France also suffered from an inhospitable climate and a conspicuous lack of the gold and silver which Europeans still tended to think of as the proper reward for 'New World' conquests. Consequently, fifty-eight years after the founding of Quebec, there were only 3,200 French colonists, most of them in and around the little capital city or the newer settlements of Trois-Rivières (established 1634) and Montreal (1642), farther up the river. During most of this initial stage, the colony fell under the authority of the Company of New France, a corporation which, like the companies that began Virginia and New Netherlands, acted in part as an arm of the State and in part as a profit-seeking enterprise.

In 1663, the young King Louis XIV dissolved the Company of New France and took over direct rule of Canada through his energetic minister of marine, Jean-Baptiste Colbert. Government administration within the colony was integrated and rationalized, and it was brought under the regular supervision of the minister in France. Louis and Colbert were embarked on a far-reaching program to bolster France's national strength by revitalizing the kingdom's trade and industry, as well as its overseas empire. The revolution in colonial governance was only one small part of a much larger plan encompassing France and its possessions in North America and the Caribbean. In Canada, this entailed not only political reorganization, but a massive campaign to build up the demographic, military, and economic strength of the colony. Through the 1660s and into the early 1670s, the government of Louis XIV poured money, soldiers, and settlers into the open funnel of the St Lawrence, with the result that Canada rapidly changed from a base camp for missionaries, traders, and explorers into something more like a European community, a 'New France' in the full sense of the term. The wheat farms of a Canadian peasantry lined the banks of the St Lawrence. Urban society was dominated, as in France, by merchants, religious orders, and aristocrats. The colony's laws, government, and land-tenure system all mirrored those of the mother country.

There were, nevertheless, differences, most notably Canada's significant aboriginal population. Quite apart from the overwhelming Native presence to the north and west of the Laurentian settlements, there were recently established Amerindian villages on the doorsteps of Quebec and Montreal. Just as French colonists were landing at the wharfs of Quebec during the immigration mini-boom of the 1660s and 1670s, Canada's aboriginal population was also bolstered with the arrival of immigrants from the south. The society which took shape through these convergent movements of people was thus a composite, with a predominantly French character and an important Amerindian element.

The history of New France was an eventful one, punctuated by wars against the Iroquois through much of the seventeenth century, and against the English in intermittent, but ever more intense, conflicts between 1689 and 1713, and from 1745 until the fall of New France in 1760.

Government policies changed, laws were instituted, economic cycles of depression and prosperity succeeded one another, explorers charted unknown regions, leaders rose and fell.

These developments can be traced in any of a dozen standard works in the field. They find little place in this book, however, which restricts itself to the more enduring characteristics of life in the Laurentian colony. The aim here is to describe, in their essential features, the 'frameworks of ordinary life' – birth, death, marriage, food, work, personal identities, race, class, and so on – during the century extending from the royal intervention of the 1660s, when a fully formed colonial society first emerged, until the end of French rule. There is a danger in such a descriptive approach that politics, conflict, and other dynamics of change will be slighted in a portrait that exaggerates harmony and stability. I hope I have avoided the pitfalls of this placid variety of social history, though I do recognize that a truly comprehensive work would have to give much more attention to change over time and include more details on crime, justice, religion, popular politics, the impact of war, and a thousand other topics. However, the fact is that only so much can be covered in a slim volume intended to introduce students to a large subject.

In attempting to make sense of the social history of New France, I take my place in a long line of interpreters stretching back to the nineteenth century and beyond. French-Canadian historians, from François-Xavier Garneau in the 1840s to Guy Frégault in the 1960s, tended to view the French regime from a nationalist perspective. They discerned in its history the birth of a nation: orderly, pious, and perpetually beleaguered by external enemies. Great men strode through the pages of their accounts, but it was the people – that is to say, the white, French-Canadian people – whose destiny was of central concern. It was their sorry fate to be abandoned by France and conquered by Britain – to be the tragic victims of the global politics of imperialism. English-language historians also tended to look at the people of New France mainly from the point of view of their role in colonization, war, and conquest. For many years, the most influential writings were those of Francis Parkman, a New England historian of the Victorian era. Parkman's great epic account portrayed the struggle between France and Britain as essentially a moral conflict, one pitting the forces of absolutism against those of liberty. Far from being an innocent victim of imperial machinations, early French Canada was intimately involved in the drama. For Parkman, almost every aspect of New France society bore the imprint of a despotic State and an overweening Church: the colony was fatally flawed, and therefore destined by Providence for inevitable defeat.

Later generations of historians in the Parkman tradition, both American and English Canadian, tended to treat the society of New France as fundamentally defective. More politely sensitive to the point of view of French Canadians, they tended to express their criticisms less baldly than the outspoken Bostonian. The approach was nevertheless pathological, with inquiries working back from the Conquest and attempting to discover the basic flaw in the French colonization project. Where did the weakness lie? these historians wondered. Was it some inadequacy on the part of the bourgeoisie: poverty? incompetence? a lack of entrepreneurial spirit? Were the habitants (agrarian settlers) at fault for their lacklustre farming practices? Was labour in short supply, or simply deficient in skill? Perhaps the fur trade, with a lure derived from its association with the wilderness and with aboriginal 'savagery,' distracted colonists from the serious business of life. The answers provided by the English-language historical literature varied, but the question was always the same: what went wrong with New France? In recent years, W.J. Eccles has elaborated an inverted version of the Parkman thesis, one which tries to put a positive construction on every authoritarian feature of the French regime.

While English-language historiography still tends to read back from policies and leadership to social realities, a new generation of French-Canadian researchers is more inclined to focus directly and exclusively on society itself. Instead of asking why New France fell, they ask how people lived there. Generally their belief is that material circumstances played a greater role than the imperial vision of Colbert or the corruption of Governor Frontenac. These historians – foremost among them, Louise Dechêne – choose their sources in accord with this perspective. Dechêne's studies, based primarily on notarial deeds, parish registers, and land records, are less reliant on the letters and reports of government officials and Church dignitaries, the sort of descriptive materials from an élite perspective which historians used to depend upon. She concludes that Canada had an *ancien régime* social configuration fundamentally similar to that of France. My own interpretation owes a great deal to the research of this last group of historians and it shares their perspective on New France society in many of its aspects. Although I am perhaps less inclined than they to accord privileged status to economic factors, I do agree with their emphasis on the frameworks of ordinary life.

Traditionally, the social history of French-regime Canada has been a story about white men, with women, blacks, and Natives cast in a secondary role. Researchers working their way against the grain of the sources are now busy trying to unearth evidence about these marginalized groups. Much remains to be done, but, in the meantime, this book incorporates the results of recently published studies, and consequently it goes much further than previous surveys of the field in including all the people of New France within its purview.

The People of New France also reflects my desire to present the French regime on its own terms, rather than as a prelude to something else. Of course it is foolish to think that one can ever describe another era entirely 'on its own terms,' as though the people of that time spoke with one harmonious voice and as though it were transparently intelligible to the present. All the same, we need to make an effort to look at seventeenth- and eighteenth-century Canada, as much as possible, as it was, rather than as an imperfect version of what it should have been or as an embryo of what it would be. This book therefore represents an attempt to liberate one portion of the past from the dead hand of the present. It tries to bring to the fore the way of life, the outlook and mentality, of the French immigrant, the Kahnawaké Mohawk, the merchant, and the servant girl. These will be presented, not as symptoms of some metaphysical fatal flaw, not as foreshadowings of defeat or starting-points for the elaboration of an enduring national character, but as primary objects worthy of our attention in and of themselves. The inhabitants of these pages are quite remote from their descendants in present-day Quebec, or from anyone else living in the late twentieth century for that matter. Therein lies their interest.

1

Population

1658

Baptized on the first of November was Henry, son of Eloy Jary dit La Haye, wheelwright, and of Jeanne Merrin his wife. The godfather was Henry Perrin, habitant, the godmother Elizabeth Bobinet, wife of Paul Benoist dit Le Nivernois, carpenter.

Henry Jary may be one of the obscure 'little people' of history, but the major events of his life – birth, marriage, children, death – did not go unnoticed or unrecorded. A religious ceremony marked each of these milestones, and the priest involved conscientiously noted the particulars in the pages of his parish register. The parish registers of New France contain, in all, approximately 300,000 entries describing all the Catholic baptisms, weddings, and funerals celebrated in Canada from 1621 to 1760. Together they constitute an unrivalled source for population studies: not only are these documents amazingly accurate and complete, but hardly any have been lost through the ravages of war, revolution, and fire, as is the case in so many European countries. Unlike the future United States, where vital registration was carried out with varying degrees of negligence by the different churches and sects, New France had a uniform system based on the Catholic Church's monopoly position. The main purpose of this elaborate record-keeping was to guard against bigamy and consanguineous marriage (which at that time could include some fairly remote kin and pseudo-kin connections), but the State also had an interest in this information and required the Church to supply it with a copy of all parish registers.

Modern historical demographers constitute another beneficiary of the care the clergy took with their parish registers. Through the techniques of 'family reconstitution,' demographers at the University of Montreal have processed this raw material and entered it into their computer data banks. Essentially they assemble the scattered entries for each inhabitant of the colony (not as easy a procedure as it sounds, given the movement of people, the prevalence of nicknames, and the lack of uniform spelling) and group these in families, so that they can calculate, to the day, such measures as the age at which an individual marries, gives birth, and dies. With data of this sort for the entire French population, the Montreal demographers have been able to perform refined analyses of fertility, mortality, and marital behaviour. Thanks, then, to New France's exceptional primary sources, as well as to modern Quebec's achievements in the science of population studies, early French Canada has become a highly developed demographic laboratory. Some of the resulting findings about how the colonial population grew will be reviewed below, but first let us look at immigration, a subject on which the parish registers have little to say.

Although the colony's human population grew mainly through natural increase, it did require a certain amount of immigrant 'seed stock.' In all, about 27,000 French people came to Canada over the century and a half preceding the Conquest and, of these, perhaps two-thirds (mostly soldiers, government administrators, and contract workers) returned home without leaving descendants in the colony. This suggests that today's 6 million French Canadians can all trace their ancestry to some 10,000 original immigrants. Given the fact that Canada was France's principal settlement colony and that France was by far the most populous nation of

Europe at the time, this figure for total immigration seems surprisingly small, especially when we note that the British colonies that later became the United States received more than 1 million immigrants, most of them from a country with a quarter of France's population. Certainly there was no shortage of grinding poverty in *ancien régime* France, and a move across the Atlantic would have improved most people's material prospects substantially. Why, then, did so few take the plunge? The answer lies in a combination of 'pull factors' (Canada's attraction to potential immigrants), 'push factors' (France's tendency to generate emigrants), and government efforts to channel and regulate the movement of people.

In the mother country, the image of New France was hardly paradisical. The severity of the winter climate was well known and the horrors of war with the Iroquois had been widely publicized by Jesuit missionaries. Government efforts to boost the colony's population by bringing over men bound as indentured servants or soldiers had the effect of associating emigration and servitude in the popular mind. 'Canada has always been regarded as a country at the end of the world,' wrote an official, 'and as an exile that might pass for a [sentence] of civil death.' A party of would-be colonists passing through a small town in Normandy once provoked a riot on the part of townspeople who, refusing to believe the travellers were leaving France voluntarily, insisted on 'rescuing' them from the colonial exile awaiting them. The dangers of Canadian life were exaggerated, and the economic advantages, especially for the peasant masses, were insufficiently appreciated, but the fact remains that the basic standard of living, though higher than that of the old country, was not dramatically better.

Canada's poor image was not the only reason for the meagre flow of transatlantic migration. The fact is that French people of the seventeenth and eighteenth centuries tended to stay in France, not only resisting the chilly charms of New France, but showing little inclination to move to any other part of the world. The English, the Scots, even the Germans, who possessed no state, and therefore no colonies of their own, were much more apt to emigrate. These other nations do not seem to have been poorer or more over-populated than France; why, then, did so many of their inhabitants uproot themselves while the French shunned colonial exile? This is really a question for European social historians, but my own hunch is that this stay-at-home quality stemmed primarily from the relatively powerful situation of France's peasantry. Peasants formed the majority throughout Europe at this time and, in some countries – notably the British Isles – they were quite vulnerable and liable to be thrown off the land through processes of enclosure or eviction. Swelling the ranks of the urban unemployed, these dislocated farming people helped fuel the demand for overseas emigration. In France, by way of contrast, peasants had managed to maintain a more secure hold over the land, and landlords had less ability to rid themselves of 'surplus' tenants. Inheritance practices may also have acted to discourage emigration. The tendency in *ancien régime* France was for property to be divided equally among all the heirs, giving everyone a stake, no matter how small, in the family home. In other countries, the law often allowed for greater inequality among heirs, so that some children would inherit the parents' property, while others would be driven to seek their fortunes far from home.

In addition to these socio-economic 'push' and 'pull' factors, migration to New France was also affected by government regulation, notably the policy of excluding Huguenots (French Protestants). The Huguenots were one element of French society who did emigrate in large numbers, particularly after the revocation (1685) of the Edict of Nantes ended official toleration of their religion. Hundreds of thousands of them took refuge in other parts of Europe, as well as in Britain's North American colonies, but they were prohibited by law from settling in New France. The result was that, for a time, there were more French speakers (all of them Huguenots) in New York than in Canada. Thus religious politics played a part in blocking the flow of one major category of potential settlers, though how large a part is impossible to say, since we cannot assume that many Protestants would have wished to live in Canada, even if they were allowed. On the other hand, France's government did contribute to the movement of Catholics to the colony through a variety of shipping regulations and subsidies. Accordingly, the heaviest flow of population to New France occurred in the 1660s and 1670s, when Louis XIV's government was engaged in a lavish program of colonial development and subsidized immigration. Even so, arrivals numbered only about 250 per year during those decades of peak immigration.

Throughout the French regime, the typical French immigrant was poor, male, and unattached. Few crossed the Atlantic as couples or in family groups, though many individuals came in the footsteps of a brother or a relative of some sort. Not usually the poorest of the poor, they seem to have been worryingly close to indigence at the time of embarkation. Almost half came from cities, more from Paris than any other single locality, though many of these rootless urbanites had been born in the country and had only recently moved to the city. Even so, the colonial emigrants formed an exceptionally urban group in a country that was predominantly rural and agrarian, and if we can believe the occupational titles they claimed, most were craftsmen and few had an agricultural background. All the provinces of France contributed to the peopling of Canada, but the bulk of migrants came from the western part of the kingdom, especially the Atlantic port of La Rochelle and its hinterland, as well as Paris, Rouen, and the Perche.

Most of these male immigrants arrived at Quebec in some form of bondage. A few were convicted criminals, or victims of a 'lettre de cachet,' exiled to the colony by judicial order. Much more numerous – indeed, the majority of all seventeenth-century immigrants – were the 'engagés' (indentured servants), workers who contracted to serve in Canada for a three-year term in return for food and lodging, a small salary, and return passage across the ocean. Their masters were commonly settlers, merchants, or religious communities, but their services could be bought, sold, or rented. *Engagés* performed much of the colony's heavy labour in the early years, unloading ships, constructing buildings, and clearing the land for farming. They could not marry, nor could they conduct trade on their own account, and, if they tried to escape, they could face severe criminal punishment: flogging, branding, or even death. Not surprisingly, many *engagés* chose to return to France at the end of their terms, but about half opted to stay in the colony, merging into the colonial peasantry or embarking for the western interior in pursuit of the fur trade.

In the eighteenth century, the colonial military garrison became the most important source of French settlers. The men (that is, those below officer rank) of the *troupes de la marine* were virtually all recruited in France, most from among the marginal and desperate elements of the cities of the kingdom. 'Racolage,' the use of subterfuge and coercion, up to and including kidnapping, was a common, though unacknowledged, recruitment technique, and so we have no way of knowing how many soldiers came to Canada voluntarily. The colonial authorities generally awarded a number of discharges every year to men who undertook to marry and settle in the colony permanently, and since the normal term of enlistment was essentially unlimited, men were glad to leave the service on these terms.

Whereas soldiers and *engagés* account for the bulk of male immigration, the largest number of women immigrants came as 'king's daughters' (*filles du roi*), the term historians have attached to the young women who arrived between 1663 and 1673 as part of the government program of subsidized female immigration. At this time French men of marriageable age outnumbered single French women six to one in Canada, and administrators were intent on giving a boost to procreation by balancing the sex ratio. Of course, potential wives might have been found closer to hand, but they were all Native women and, although there had been talk earlier in the seventeenth century of encouraging the marriage of French men and Native women, the idea had been quietly dropped by the 1660s. Thus the 'king's daughters' program represented a racial reorientation as much as a demographic developmentalist agenda. At any rate, about 770 women came, most of them aged twenty-five or under, the majority orphans ('enfants du roi'). Even more than male immigrants, the women who came to New France were of urban background: the bulk of them came from one gigantic hospital/asylum in Paris, La Salpêtrière. They crossed the sea, landed at Quebec, and then plunged straight into the life of colonial society with head-spinning rapidity: within weeks of arrival, most had chosen a mate from among the eager bachelors, had married, and were on their way to a pioneer farm.

A footnote on the legend of the king's daughters may be in order at this point. From the seventeenth century down to the present day, their situation has given rise to lurid fantasies in sexist minds. Contemporary wits loved to refer to them as 'merchandise' and declared that they were certainly prostitutes plucked from the streets of Paris and placed on display before an audience of rough and randy habitants. (Never considered for a moment was the possibility that the women might have been the 'shoppers,' and the men the objects of scrutiny, in these matrimonial encounters.) Such a reaction is unremarkable in the context of the times. These were, after all, young women who were not subject to parental authority (though they were chaperoned), nor were they enclosed within a secure institution; furthermore, they contracted marriage directly rather than through the mediation of a family. Thus, they touched the edges of sexual disorder, and that made them, according to the dominant view of the time, honorary prostitutes. The only surprising aspect of this story is the response of modern writers who swallow this ancient yarn about 'bad girls' on the matrimonial block or, just as naïvely, set off in chivalrous pursuit of reliable evidence on the moral attainments of the king's daughters. Few seem to recognize the legend for what it is: an interesting indicator of *ancien régime* gender ideology.

Though overseas immigration to New France was virtually 100 per cent French, there was also an important flow of Native people into the St Lawrence valley in the seventeenth century. These were, of course, not immigrants in the conventional sense of the term, as they were relocating within territory they clearly considered their own and, even when they settled close to the French and accepted the authority of the king, they often retained a high degree of sovereign autonomy. The fact remains that many Mohawks and other Five Nations Iroquois moved from their villages in what is now upstate New York to the Montreal area. Most came during the time of peace, roughly 1667–84. Abenakis from northern New England, not to mention Huron refugees and Algonquins from the northwest, also quit their homelands to come and bolster the population of the Canadian settlements. The records are far from complete, and there was always considerable back-and-forth movement, and so it is hard to quantify this Native 'immigration.' Certainly it numbered in the thousands. In the Montreal region, newly arrived Natives probably outnumbered newly arrived French through most of the second half of the seventeenth century.

As time passed, the Native proportion of the 'Canadian' population declined. (The reference here is to residents of the St Lawrence settlements only; the rest of the territory we now call 'Canada' remained entirely Native.) Native demographic behaviour, like Native migration patterns, cannot be measured precisely, but it does seem clear that this element of the population did not grow as quickly as the French, and the reasons are not hard to fathom. Even after the devastating die-offs that accompanied the initial exposure to imported germs and viruses, aboriginal peoples long remained vulnerable to European diseases. Year after year, the missionary reports tell of babies and children carried off to heaven after falling ill with unnamed fevers. Christian Iroquois and Abenakis who survived to adulthood were usually better equipped to resist disease, but the men among them tended instead to be cut down in the wars they waged on behalf of the king of France. As a consequence of fearsome military casualties, the Native villages of Canada were filled with widows, and birth rates therefore remained low. This depressed fertility was offset to some extent by the practice of adopting French-Canadian orphans and bastards; prisoners of war from the south – Amerindians and Anglo-American colonists – were also integrated into the local population.

The number of French people in the St Lawrence valley expanded rapidly and steadily. There were about 3,000 colonists in the mid-1660s, when the government began its great program of colonial development; by the early 1680s, after a major spurt of immigration, the figure had risen to some 10,000; when the British took over seven decades later, there were perhaps 75,000 French Canadians. The numbers are quite small, but the growth rate, with its doubling every generation, was phenomenal by the standards of both aboriginal North America and pre-industrial Europe. Moreover, this rate of increase was mostly the product of natural growth. Immigration played an important role only in priming the demographic pump; otherwise, it was basically a matter of babies outnumbering corpses.

Various interesting explanations have been advanced to account for the procreative achievements of early French Canada. There is, for example, the theory that government populationist measures which rewarded large families and penalized bachelors made the difference. But private behaviour is rarely that susceptible to administrative manipulation, as proved by the fact that French-Canadian birth rates remained just as high after the British conquest, when official efforts to promote fertility were a thing of the past.

Or was it the Catholic Church, notorious today for its pro-family, anti–birth control stance, that persuaded the faithful to go forth and multiply? The fact is that marital contraception was not used to a significant degree *anywhere* before the middle of the eighteenth century. And Catholicism was not particularly natalist or pro-family in that historical context; to the contrary, in this area it differed from Protestantism mainly in exalting celibacy. If religion does not hold the key, was there, then, some earthy French-Canadian spirit at work (traditionally a favourite fantasy of English Canadians who liked to consider themselves further removed from the raw impulses of nature), perhaps accentuated by the influence of Quebec's long, cold winter nights? This theory comes up against the fact that the upright Puritans of seventeenth-century New England seem to have had about the same birth rate as the supposedly lusty habitants of New France. Sad to say, though lust has everything to do with population growth in general, it tells us nothing about why some populations grow faster than others. On this subject, cold statistics are more helpful than hot blood or cold weather.

Analysing French Canada's population growth and placing it against an international backdrop, Quebec historical demographers have found that the colony, in essence, followed a high-growth variant of the standard pre-industrial European demographic regime. Throughout the European and colonial world of the seventeenth and early eighteenth centuries, fertility (the incidence of births in a given population) and mortality (the prevalence of death) were high by modern standards. Furthermore, births outside marriage were fairly rare, and contraceptive practices played no statistically significant part in shaping families. Phrased in general terms, these observations would apply equally to Old and to New France: the differences lay in the specific details. Basically the colonial population had rather higher fertility and lower mortality than that of the mother country, but its behaviour was fundamentally similar in most respects.

Birth rates in New France hovered around fifty-five per thousand, which is to say that for every thousand people, an average of fifty-five babies were born each year. This is at the high end of the scale for pre-industrial populations, substantially higher than the birth rates – most of which ranged between thirty and forty per thousand – then common in western Europe. Another way to look at fertility is to say that married women in the colony tended to have a baby approximately once every two years until they reached menopause. From marriage to about age forty-five, pregnancies succeeded one another at a regular pace without any sign of significant attempts to limit conception. This relentless cycle of pregnancy and childbirth may seem remarkable from today's standpoint, but it was not at all exceptional in the context of the times. In that pre-industrial era, married women throughout the European and colonial world tended to have babies on the same two-year rhythm. Obviously, individual lives followed different paths, but when data are assembled for substantial numbers of families, the overall pattern is nearly universal across the 'western world.' That being the case, how can Canada's birth rate have been so much higher than that of France and the rest of western Europe? The answer lies mainly in the area of marriage practices.

In Europe, socio-economic conditions were not entirely favourable to matrimony. In the effective absence of birth control, marriage inevitably meant children, and consequently an obligation to support dependents, something many people at the lower end of the economic scale could not undertake, particularly in their teens, or even their twenties. The poor often had to wait until their thirties before they could hope to support a family; others never did find the wherewithal to marry, and went to the grave earning their single pittance as a maid, soldier, or lackey. Many sons and daughters of the élite were also effectively denied a mate, not because of poverty, but through the operation of family economic strategies. Then there were the broken marriages, the great majority interrupted by death rather than divorce: every woman widowed before the onset of menopause was one fewer producer of children. That is, unless she married again, but in France, older men, whether bachelors or widowers, tended to prefer virginal brides, and so the widows, in a great many cases, remained widows. The result was European birth rates well below the population's biological capacity, their levels governed, not by 'family planning' as we have come to know it, but by economic limitations and social inequalities.

In New France, by way of contrast, almost everyone got married, a few priests and nuns excepted, and the primary reason was that the economy offered fewer obstacles and more incentives to family formation. If there was no better way to earn a living, one could almost always obtain some land to farm and feed a family. Indeed, it was difficult to imagine pioneering without a mate and without the prospect of children. In comparison with France, there was less need to wait, and consequently people married rather young. In the mid-1600s when (white) women were in short supply, girls came under great pressure to marry the moment they reached physical maturity; the average age of first-time brides before 1660 was fifteen. This was a temporary situation, however. With the influx of 'king's daughters' and the growth of a Canadian-born female population, the ratio of men to women evened out and, by 1700, women had an average age of twenty-two when they married – still low by European standards, though not off the bottom end of the scale. Their spouses were rather older: the age of colonial grooms averaged twenty-eight years at this time. Marrying earlier than their European counterparts gave Canadian women effectively more child-bearing years, and the lower colonial mortality had a similar result since it meant that the child-bearing potential of fewer couples was interrupted by premature death. And when death did occur, the widows and widowers of New France tended to find another mate and marry again, usually after only a minimal period of mourning. With brides marrying young and widows remarrying promptly, a high proportion of the population was, at any given time, currently married and busily engaged in the production of biannual offspring.

Thus the high fertility of early French Canada can be explained through the encounter of pre-industrial European demographic patterns with 'New World' economic conditions. Religious teachings, the nationalist 'revenge of the cradles,' and cold winters hardly need to be mentioned. Indeed, other European settler societies, such as that of colonial New England, seem to have had similarly high levels of fertility ('seem' because the sources are less complete and reliable than those of New France). The real peculiarity of French Canada's demographic history lies in the fact that birth rates remained high long after the pioneer conditions of abundant land had disappeared. Whereas the data suggest that New Englanders were beginning to practise some form of birth control in the decades before the American Revolution, rural Quebeckers kept having babies with little sign of contraceptive practices right up into the twentieth century. Social historians are struggling to explain the late arrival of the modern fertility decline in French Canada, but for the pre-Conquest period that interests us, the consistently vigorous birth rate is much less mysterious.

And what of mortality? Population growth is determined, after all, by the prevalence of death as well as by the pace of childbirth. By and large, the people of New France were healthy and well fed, and consequently, for those who survived the perils of infancy, the prospects of a long life were fairly good. Implicitly contrasting Canada with France's tropical colonies in the West Indies, one visitor wrote: 'There is no climate in the world that is healthier; there are no diseases specific to the country; those that I have seen there were brought by French ships. There are nevertheless some women afflicted by goitres, which are caused, they say, by the melting of the snows.' Endemic sickness may not have been a major threat, but Canadians none the less knew that they could be struck down at any moment. Seventeenth-century priests sometimes (on 4,587 occasions, to be precise) recorded the cause of death in their parish registers, and an analysis of these entries reveals a surprising number of accidental and violent deaths. (The latter were, of course, far more likely to be noted in the records than routine losses.) We read of 51 people felled by lightning bolts; 299 war casualties; 71 crushed by trees and other falling objects; 37 frozen to death; 69 killed by fire; and, most remarkably, 1,302 deaths by drowning. This last figure reflects the importance, as well as the dangers, of travel by canoe, bateau, and ship in this riverside colony. (No wonder Saint Anne, with her shrine at Beaupré and her habit of coming to the aid of mariners in distress, was such a favourite among colonial Catholics.) Equally striking, in so far as we can rely on this highly selective data, are the very low figures for suicide (13) and murder (15). In spite of all these hazards, however, the mortality of adults and older children remained moderate by pre-industrial standards.

Babies did not fare so well. Approximately one out of every five newborns in seventeenth-century Canada died before reaching its first birthday. By the eighteenth century, that figure had risen to one in four, placing the colony somewhere near the middle of the range of infant-mortality figures then prevailing in Europe. In normal years, then, life was somewhat more secure in New France than in France, but, particularly when infant deaths are taken into account, Canada's edge was not huge.

It was the abnormal times, the years of famines and epidemics, when death stalked the land, that tended to keep down population growth in pre-industrial Europe. Seventeenth-century France suffered a succession of terrible die-offs; most were local or regional in scope, but the cumulative effect was to prevent any long-term growth in the kingdom's population, even though births regularly exceeded deaths by a substantial margin in normal years. Food shortages lay at the root of most of these disasters, and when poor weather or some other accident destroyed harvests, thousands of peasants, already living just on the right side of the threshold of subsistence, were in danger of slipping into the abyss. Disease usually delivered the *coup de grâce*, but it was hunger that weakened the population's resistance. The white settler population of New France, by way of contrast, enjoyed virtually complete exemption from serious mortality crises. Since they were so few in relation to the resources of North America, they lived much farther from the brink of disaster than did their European cousins. This is not to say that there were never food shortages in the St Lawrence colony, for indeed grain crops did fail here, about as often as they did in the old country. But Canadian habitants were usually able to survive agricultural emergencies by turning to fish, wild fruits, and other products of nature that would not have been available in significant quantities in the overcrowded French countryside. Real starvation hit the colony only once, and that was at the very end of the French regime, when the British war of conquest produced a serious famine.

'Mortality crises' certainly were a feature of seventeenth-century life in eastern Canada, but they came mainly in the form of epidemics rather than famines, and their chosen victims were Native people. As mentioned earlier, Old World pathogens struck down aboriginals in appalling numbers, to the extent that the famous crises of seventeenth-century France seem paltry in comparison. However, the French settlers of Canada were, for the most part, protected by the antibodies built up by their ancestors from the deadly effects of the diseases which ravaged their Iroquoian and Algonquian neighbours. This is not to say that early French Canada was entirely exempt from epidemics. From time to time, ships would arrive from France or the West Indies carrying smallpox or some variety of 'fever' and, in spite of rudimentary public-health measures, sickness often spread to the resident population. In 1685, the nuns of the *hôtel-Dieu* received the typhus-stricken crew of a ship that had just moored in the harbour of Quebec: 'There were so many sick in this ship that soon the wards, the chapel, the barns, the chicken coop and all the hospital grounds, wherever a place could be found for them – even tents were put up in the yard – were filled. We redoubled our efforts to serve them and they had great need of our help – fevers, terrible and burning, delirium and much scurvy. There came into our hospital more than three hundred sick.' Epidemics occurred more frequently in the eighteenth century than the seventeenth, in part because the towns were becoming more crowded and the maritime traffic heavier; war years, when soldiers and sailors disembarked in large numbers, were the worst. And yet, for all the suffering they caused, these epidemics seldom spread far beyond the port city and they never took a demographically significant toll on the settler population of New France. All in all, then, early French Canada was spared the worst effects of both disease and famine. The absence of serious crisis mortality, coupled with colonial marriage patterns favouring high fertility, largely explains why this population grew so much faster than other pre-industrial populations, most notably that of old-regime Europe.

It starts with a handful of newcomers from France and from Iroquoia. Once installed along the St Lawrence, they had children, and their children had children, in numbers that increased geometrically with each succeeding generation. When Guillemette Hébert died in 1684, she was mourned by no fewer than 143 children, grandchildren, and great-grandchildren. By 1730 her descendants numbered 689. And hers was not the most fecund settler family, though it was at the high end of the scale. This example serves to illustrate a basic fact about New France's demographic history: expansive natural growth, rather than massive immigration, was the main force populating this colony.

But where did all these people go, and how did they earn a living in their raw adopted homeland? The short answer, in eight cases out of ten, was that they colonized the land, built themselves farms, and drew their livelihood from the soil.

2

Life on the Land

It is the spring of 1670 and a young couple is setting out from Montreal to take possession of a patch of forest twelve kilometres east of the little town. Recently married, they have already had their names entered in the estate rolls of the Sulpicians, the order of priests who control the giant seigneury encompassing the entire island of Montreal. The woman – let us call her Marie – is a nineteen-year-old settler's daughter, and her husband – he can be named Pierre – is a former *engagé*, somewhat older than Marie. When he left his native Saintonge more than three years earlier, Pierre had fully intended to return to France on completing his service, but he had been captivated, more by Marie than by the charms of colonial life, and he decided to stay on and make Canada his home. The newlyweds have a good idea of the challenges before them and they have made their preparations carefully. Pierre carries a sack of flour, an axe, and a pickaxe, all purchased with his *engagé* earnings, while Marie leads part of her dowry down the path in the form of a cow (her brother will deliver the bed later). At last they reach the little clearing, with its rustic cabin, near the river at *côte* Ste-Anne. Pierre had managed to put together this shelter with thin tree trunks sharpened at one end. These he had pounded into the ground to form a rectangle of vertical posts 4.5 metres by 6.0; the roof he fashioned from branches supporting large chunks of bark;

sods fill the gaps between the posts. Marie and Pierre place their things on the earth floor of their dwelling, and soon the long process of transforming forest into farmland begins.

The first order of business is to fell the maples, pines, and oaks and expand the original clearing. Pierre cuts the straightest logs into six-metre lengths and rolls them to one side, where they will stay until he can find the time to assemble them into a new house. Weeks later, there is a good-sized opening to the sky, and the couple must burn the remaining brush and clear the ground as best they can with axe and pick and human muscle. A summer's work might produce one or two *arpents* of clearing (an *arpent* is roughly equivalent to an acre, or one-third of a hectare) ready to be tilled by pick in the fall. Here and there, a great tree too thick to chop has been girdled and left to die, and many of the larger stumps and rocks still dot the little 'field,' leaving patches of rich earth to be sown in the spring with Iroquoian crops: corn, beans, and squash. Meanwhile, Pierre spends the winter clearing more land and, along with his neighbours, helps to push the ragged forest front farther back from the river with every passing year. After a few years, he and Marie may be able to scrape together a little money from occasional wage work, and from sales of firewood, eggs, and produce in Montreal; that, and some borrowed capital, allows them to purchase a pair of oxen to drag out the boulders and rotten stumps, transforming their pock-marked clearing into a field. Pierre hitches up his two-wheeled plough, largely home-made, and starts to cut furrows like a real French *laboureur*. Impatient to reconnect with their European heritage, they have already pushed North American crops into the background in favour of the Old World staple, wheat. Pierre now brings ample supplies of flour back from the seigneurial mill, and the couple dines on good white bread, with none of the 'inferior' dark grains that impoverished European peasants have to settle for.

Five years and three babies after their wedding, Pierre and Marie also have a new house. Endless trimming with the axe had flattened the round sides of the logs until Pierre had enough squared 'pieces' to assemble a neat log building in the emerging French-Canadian style of 'pièce-sur-pièce.' Their original rough cabin now houses the farm animals: a cow, the oxen, a sow, a dozen chickens. Marie is in charge of this little flock, as well as the kitchen garden, where cabbages, onions, and other vegetables grow, not to mention the family's supply of tobacco. Marie's efforts, punctuated by recurrent pregnancy and childbirth, are multifaceted. Less visible than Pierre's in the records, they are no less vital to the family's survival. Man and woman, aided more and more by their children as they grow older, as well as by the occasional *coup de main* from neighbours and relatives, gradually expand their clearing, improve their house, fence their fields, maintain the front road, and endeavour to get their grown sons and daughters launched in life. Hard though their life may be, they have, by about the time Marie turns forty, achieved something important. They have what their peasant ancestors always aspired to: independence, the ability to live on what they could provide with their own labour, their own equipment, their own land.

This composite profile, adapted from Louise Dechêne's wonderfully rich *Habitants and Merchants in Seventeenth-Century Montreal*, describes an early stage in the emergence of the French-Canadian 'habitant' class, a term which in the Canadian context came to designate landowning cultivators or peasants. We have to imagine this family multiplied a thousand times, building their farms along the banks of the St Lawrence all around Montreal, as well as east and west of Quebec on both sides of the river. Each succeeding generation of habitants was larger than the previous one, and so population growth drove along a continuous process of colonization that brought more and more territory under the plough throughout the French regime and beyond. Although there was some tendency to cluster around the two cities, settlement always stayed close to the water. Gaps between Montreal and Quebec filled in rapidly, so that, by the eighteenth century, there were two virtually unbroken ribbons of farms stretching some 400 kilometres from a point just upriver from Montreal to a straggling end well beyond Quebec. Colonization was also proceeding up the Richelieu and Chaudière, as well as some smaller tributaries of the St Lawrence. Near the cities, inland rows of farms were opening up behind the riverside concessions.

Throughout the history of New France, property was laid out in long, thin rectangles, usually fronting on the river and disappearing into the depths of forest behind. This oblong shape had long been typical of 'pioneer' regions of medieval Europe as it offered several advantages to new settlers. Since houses were built close together, the burden of road building was minimized and, in the Canadian case, access to the water for transportation, drinking, and fishing was maximized. Initial surveying was also simplified when a single line of stakes could designate the front corners of each lot. Apart from the fact that it was seigneurs who administered the granting of lands to would-be habitants, there was nothing particularly 'seigneurial' about this configuration. It was possible to have seigneurial tenure with irregular lots (as was the case throughout most of *ancien régime* France) or long, thin farms, but no seigneurial tenure (in the Red River colony of Western Canada, for example).

Peter Kalm, a Swedish naturalist who visited the country in the summer of 1749, was charmed by the vista as his boat passed down the St Lawrence from Montreal to Quebec: 'The country on both sides was very delightful today, and the fine state of its cultivation added greatly to the beauty of the scene. It could really be called a village, beginning at Montreal and ending at Quebec [it didn't actually end at Quebec, but that is as far as Kalm went], which is a distance of more than one hundred and eighty miles [290 kilometres], for the farmhouses are never above five arpens [300 metres] and sometimes but three apart ...' The three-day journey took him past churches and windmills, wheat fields and meadows. In the absence of inns, he stopped for the night at a habitant dwelling and, like almost every foreigner visiting French Canada, was struck by the cheerful hospitality of this colonial peasantry. Kalm was also favourably impressed by the houses themselves: 'The houses in this neighbourhood are all made of wood [i.e., squared logs]. The rooms are pretty large ... The windows are made entirely of paper. The chimney is erected in the middle of the room; that part of the room which is opposite the fire is the kitchen; that which is behind the chimney serves the people for sleeping and entertaining strangers. Sometimes there is an iron stove ... The roofs are covered with boards, and crevices and chinks [in the walls] are filled up with clay. Other farm buildings are covered with straw.' Peter Kalm's hosts were, in effect, the great-grandchildren of Pierre and Marie, and their home was basically similar to that of their ancestors, though perhaps a bit bigger, and certainly a lot warmer in winter, thanks to the use of iron stoves manufactured in the colony at the St Maurice Forges since the 1730s.

Censuses, as well as data from the files of local notaries who were often called upon to list family possessions as part of an inheritance settlement, all suggest that there was a high degree of uniformity in habitant farms. Some habitants were certainly better off than others, but destitution was as rare as opulence. Most had between 60 and 120 *arpents* of land, usually enough for an ample grain field and pasture, with a woodlot at the back to maintain a steady supply of winter fuel. If a habitant had much more land than that, the excess was probably being held in trust for a son who would take possession when he married.

In livestock holdings, too, one farm looked roughly the same as the next: the majority had two to four milk cows, as well as a pig or two, and a dozen hens. By and large, these numbers reflect the requirements of a rural family for beef, pork, eggs, and milk. By Kalm's time, many habitants also kept one or two horses, which they used instead of oxen to plough their fields. This may have been a response to the development of a road network, which allowed country people in the eighteenth century to use their horses for transportation as well as tillage. Driving their *calèches* in summer and their *carioles* in winter, habitants now travelled great distances on business and pleasure. Peter Kalm thought they had 'too many horses,' his judgment simply echoing the conventional view of the Canadian upper class with whom he consorted: if they must stray from home, peasants belong with their feet in the humble dust. Elsewhere, Kalm notes (and here again a normative judgment on social hierarchy is smuggled into a useful observation on agricultural practice) that 'every countryman commonly keeps a few sheep which supply him with as much wool as he needs to clothe himself with.' Of course, men had very little to do with sheep, but habitant women frequently clothed their families in wool from their own sheep, and linen from home-grown flax.

Rural New France was the land *par excellence* of the self-sufficient family household. The typical habitant family subsisted almost entirely on the produce of its own farm; moreover, it was able to provide for the greater part of its own material needs – housing, fuel, clothing, transportation – through its own productive efforts on its own land. This sort of self-sufficiency is basic to the way of life of peasantries and settler populations all around the pre-industrial world. Rural life in France at this time had a similar fundamental tendency, though the picture there is complicated by the fact that many country folk did not have enough land to support themselves, and therefore had to eke out a living as best they could, often sending their sons and daughters to live with richer neighbours as 'servants' (farm and household help). Comparatively easy access to land largely eliminated these complicating factors in Canada, so that, much more than in Europe, families were able to live together, work together, and subsist independently. Even the geography of settlement, featuring self-contained farms rather than the nucleated villages common in France, illustrates just how central the family farm was to the life of rural New France.

This being said, we need to add some qualifications in order to head off the misunderstandings which frequently follow recognition of this underlying pattern of habitant self-sufficiency. This was not a 'closed' agrarian system, willfully isolated from the market economy of price, exchange, and profit. Habitants always drew on the outside world for some essential supplies, such as salt and hardware, as well as a wide variety of ribbons, wine, pins, and other luxury products and, of course, they could not escape the burden of rents and tithes. This was no 'barter economy,' even though few purchases were paid for with hard cash. Habitants habitually relied on credit, short-term or long-term, but whether their debt was to a merchant, a seigneur, a relative, or a neighbour, it was recorded in monetary terms. The rural household had to have something of value – some combination of money, labour, and farm produce – to offer the world outside. We know, for example, that many habitant men from the Montreal and Trois-Rivières areas worked from time to time in the western fur trade, while some living farther east made money fishing and sealing. Women near the towns might sell some vegetables, eggs, and dairy products. There was even an urban market for grain, but it was not large, because the colonial population was so small. The colonial military garrison and the crews of visiting ships provided additional outlets for Canadian grain, but it was only after 1720 that significant opportunities appeared, with the development of Louisbourg and other markets in French North America. The eighteenth century witnessed a rising demand for Canadian wheat, and the habitants responded by growing more and more grain. All this goes to prove that the self-sufficiency of the habitant household was not absolute, nor was it impervious to market forces.

Neither was this really a 'static' rural society. On the

contrary, it was a highly dynamic configuration of household cells, each one expanding and contracting over the years as children were born and old folks died. Cells split and multiplied as young people married and forged out on their own. And, of course, every new family needed a family farm, which brings us to the topic of property inheritance. The rules of inheritance laid down by the Custom of Paris, New France's civil law, essentially called for parents' possessions to be divided equally among all their children, male and female. One might then think – and an amazing number of historians have fallen into this trap – that the high fertility of early French Canada would have led to family farms being divided and subdivided into ever-tinier fractions with each successive generation. The law only conferred a claim on each heir; it did not require the literal division of property. Consider the case of Amable Ménard and Théophile Allaire, a Richelieu valley couple married in 1753, not long after his father and her mother had died. Since both Théophile's parents were now deceased, he and his four brothers and six sisters were each entitled to twenty-three *arpents* of the family estate, as well as an equal share of the movable possessions. This was not enough land to support a family, however, and no one for a moment considered physically dismembering the farm into unviable plots this size. Instead, Théophile and Amable bought out the shares of one of his brothers and one of his sisters, older siblings already established on their own farms. They financed this purchase with Amable's inheritance from her mother. Since her father was still alive, she and her siblings had a legal claim to shares of only half the family fortune; the old man willingly turned over 370 *livres* to his daughter to extinguish her claim and regain full control over the property that, in practice, he already controlled anyway. Thus, money from the Ménard side of the family was used to purchase land from the Allaire side and, after some additional exchanges and readjustments, the young couple ended up with title to a viable habitant farm.

Economically self-sufficient and physically self-contained, habitant households were certainly not socially isolated. There was lots of visiting and socializing in the French-Canadian countryside. Especially in the winter, when chores were less pressing and when travel over the fields and the frozen rivers was easier, people gathered to celebrate weddings, New Year's Eve, and the festivals of local patron saints. Formal community institutions were largely lacking: there was no counterpart, for example, of the French rural *commune*, a municipal body set up mainly to administer tax collection. There was no *commune* in the colony because no direct taxes were levied there (which is not to say that habitants were not burdened by the State: in addition to paying tithes and seigneurial dues, they could be conscripted into military service or road-building duty, or they might see their grain requisitioned by force). About the only framework for local community life was the parish.

Parishes were only established gradually, after a given area had developed to the point where it could hope to support a resident priest (*curé*). Viewed from above, the parish looked like an authoritarian unit of administration, set up on orders from the bishop and run by his delegate, the *curé*. The latter was remunerated through the tithe, which in New France amounted to one–twenty-sixth of the grain harvest, as well as minor fees for weddings and funerals. Building a church, providing suitable housing for the priest, and collecting assessments and voluntary contributions to pay for annual expenses constituted additional responsibilities for the habitant/laity. The top-down view of the parish as an instrument of control and revenue extraction is quite misleading, however. It is true that the habitants dutifully provided a local church and rectory, as required by the clergy, but their attitude towards these buildings was far from deferential. In defiance of the view propounded by priests and bishops, rural lay people tended to act as though the church and rectory were community halls, built by and for the use of local residents. For most habitants, the church was not exclusively a sacred space, and Sunday Mass was a time of socializing as well as worship. *Curés* complained of parishioners chatting in the pews, wandering outside for a smoke during the sermon, bringing their dogs along to Mass, generally making themselves altogether too comfortable. And the rectory was never entirely the private residence of the priest. A French military engineer, recounting a visit in 1752 to a country priest, remarked that 'his house contains a large room where, as is the custom in this country, the principal residents meet, before or after the mass, to discuss the affairs of the parish.'

Most parishes in the Canadian countryside were set up at the request of the local inhabitants and, once established, served to define identities and to focus local attachments. Woe betide the bishop who interfered with the settled community arrangements by adjusting parochial boundaries or ordering the relocation of a church. Monseigneur Saint-Vallier provoked fierce protests in 1714 when he tried to rationalize parish boundaries in response to shifting patterns of settlement around St Léonard, near Montreal. An official sent to investigate the disturbances was attacked by a crowd of women, who threatened to kill him and throw his body into the swamp. Other disputes centred on the vestry and its council of elected churchwardens (*marguilliers*), always suspicious of any interference by the priest. The rural parish, like the agrarian landscape itself, was largely a creation of the habitants and, if it often became an arena of conflict pitting lay people against clergy, this should be seen as evidence of the degree to which the peasantry had attached themselves to the institution and made it their own.

And where are the seigneurs in all this? You might recall that Pierre and Marie originally received their grant of land from the Church body that controlled the seigneury (or fief) of Montreal, and yet the profile of habitant life up to this point has treated the settlers as though they were independent proprietors, developing their lands as they saw fit, buying real estate, selling produce, and passing on their property to their heirs. Habitant families, were in this sense, independent, and their land was their own; if they held secure and permanent title, no one could evict them, though they could sell their farms if they wished. And yet they paid rent, and they were 'vassals' (to use an archaic term still occasionally heard in the nineteenth century) who pledged homage to a local lord. Should we then see the habitants as *tenants* or as *proprietors*? Addressing this question will require us to look more closely at French Canada's 'seigneurial system.'

At an early stage of the colonization of Canada, the entire St Lawrence valley had been divided into large tracts and granted as 'fiefs' or 'seigneuries' to favoured individuals, usually nobles, or to ecclesiastical bodies, such as the Jesuits, the Ursulines, or, in the case of the island of Montreal, the Sulpicians. On the map, most seigneuries looked like over-sized versions of the habitant farms they contained, with several kilometres of river frontage and parallel boundary lines running back into the depths of the forest. They existed because the French government, like other colonial regimes of the time, sought to structure property relations so as to foster the emergence of a landed élite. New France's élite was primarily clerical and noble, though commoners with enough money could and did purchase fiefs from the descendants of the original grantees. And why were seigneuries coveted? They offered the promise of long-term security and aristocratic prestige and, under the right cir-cumstances, provided substantial revenues. Estate manage-ment inevitably entailed some trouble and expense for the seigneur, but, on the whole, it was the Pierres and Maries of New France who made the fiefs of the colony valuable by building up the productive capacity of their lands.

The main benefit a seigneur extracted from a habitant (or a merchant, artisan, or anyone else holding land within the fief) came in the form of rent. The rent on a given parcel of land was specified in the title deed ('concession') when the lot was first granted. Rents might be expressed in terms of money, produce, or labour (a typical ninety-*arpent* farm lot granted in the eighteenth century might owe four and one-half *livres* cash per year, plus two and one-quarter *minots* of wheat and one day's work), but, once set, they remained invariable for all time. Regardless of the ravages of time and inflation, and even though the grantee might die and the lot in question might be divided in the process of inheritance or alienated to a stranger, those ninety *arpents* would always owe the same number of *livres, minots,* and days to the current seigneur. Unlike a landlord renting out land on a limited-term lease, a seigneur had no opportunity to adjust the rent as market conditions and the value of the property changed. The main factor determining his rental revenue was simply the number of lands in the seigneury granted out to rent-paying habitants.

Canadian seigneurs did, however, enjoy other lucrative privileges. There was a mutation fine ('lods et ventes') which amounted to a sort of sales tax on real-estate transactions; the purchaser of any land in the seigneury had to pay one-twelfth the purchase price. The 'banalité' conferred a monopoly over grist-milling, so that habitants had to take their wheat to the seigneurial mill, turning over one sack of flour out of every fourteen as payment for this service. Most seigneurs also had judicial privileges, though few exercised their right to set up law courts. They were more likely to assert their rights over fishing, timber, and common pastures in an effort to extract additional payments from the settlers in their fiefs. Lax at first, when habitants were few and the fiefs of New France largely undeveloped, the seigneurial hold over the colony's agrarian economy grew stronger, and the burden on farming families heavier, as population and the value of land and grain increased. By the end of the French regime, a substantial proportion of the surplus production, that is, of the grain not needed to keep family members alive, was being siphoned off by the colony's seigneurs. All in all, seigneurial exactions did tear a significant chunk out of the habitant household economy, though they were never large enough to make seigneurs truly wealthy; the agricultural economy was too small, and the seigneurs too numerous (there may have been about 200 of them at any given time, though it is difficult to be precise since some held several fiefs and some held fractional shares of a single seigneury), for an opulent landed aristocracy to emerge.

To find great landed estates in colonial North America, we have to turn from the French to the British colonies. In New York and Prince Edward Island, for example, grantees received something much closer to full property rights to their vast domains and they could develop them more or less as they wished, extracting the land's resources themselves or, more commonly, selling or leasing farm lots to settlers. The 'feudal' property laws of early modern France, by contrast, were much more restrictive: within their fiefs, seigneurs enjoyed a variety of privileges, including the right to exact certain specified payments from the habitants, but they did not have full control over their estates. Most notably, the power of eviction was not available to them: if habitants failed to pay their rents, the seigneur's only recourse was to launch a lawsuit, like any other creditor. It is clear, then, that these were not 'landlords,' as we understand the term today or as it was employed in the British empire at the time. If this seems strange or puzzling, that may be because the basic idea of landownership itself is inherently problematic, as a moment's reflection on the subject reveals. The whole notion that a portion of the earth's surface can be 'owned' in the same sense that a shirt or a tool can be 'owned' is a culturally sanctioned fiction established in law. One does not own land because one has made it, or bought it from someone who made it. Landowners cannot take their property with them from place to place. They own it, instead, by a legal convention which pretends that land is like a truly personal possession. And nothing illustrates this point better than the situation of the seigneurs of New France. Owning a seigneury did not entail owning the soil within its boundaries: what was owned was a bundle of specific and limited rights over productive activity within that territory.

Certainly seigneurs did not own the habitants residing on their fiefs. There was no serfdom in New France and, in this respect, as in most others, Canadian seigneurialism resembled that of seventeenth-century France, where seigneurs no longer told peasants where they could travel and whom they could marry. Personally free, habitants were nevertheless subject to economic exploitation; moreover, their control over their own lands was less than absolute. Who, then, should we regard as the owner of Pierre and Marie's farm: the habitant family who reaped its harvests and who could sell it or pass it on to their children as they wished? Or the Sulpician order who collected rent and who reserved the right to cut timber or build a mill there? The answer is that, under seigneurial tenure, both parties were owners, but neither was a proprietor in a complete and absolute sense. Instead, the attributes of ownership were divided.

Up to now, we have been looking only at the French-Canadian habitants, but the St Lawrence valley was home to another, quite distinct, category of agrarian settlers. The Iroquois who came to settle beside the French on the mountain behind Montreal and across the river, at Kahnawaké, had built themselves bark-covered longhouses and begun clearing fields to plant their traditional crops: corn, together with squash and beans. A few cows, pigs, and chickens made their appearance in the Christian Native villages, but otherwise European agriculture made little impression. Growing the corn, harvesting and preserving it, and preparing the meals of boiled *sagamite* remained a strictly female responsibility. The crops grew on artificial hillocks, which the women, working together in teams to pass the time more pleasantly, cultivated with digging sticks. The men were frequently away on war parties in the summer, an activity which brought some extra income to the community in the form of booty and government rewards, not to mention adoptable prisoners. In winter, most people departed in small bands of one or two families for hunting-grounds on the Ottawa River or some other distant location; this seasonal migration provided a welcome change from an otherwise monotonous diet and it helped ease the pressure on limited stocks of corn. It does seem that the agriculture on Canada's Native reserves was less bountiful than on the original Huron and Iroquois lands. The Iroquoian peoples normally practised a form of 'slash and burn' agriculture whereby clearings cut from the forest (land clearing is where the men made their contribution) were farmed intensively for as long as their virginal fertility lasted. After ten to twenty years, the fields would be abandoned and a new patch of forest cleared some distance away. This system – essentially a form of crop rotation with very long fallow periods – required lots of elbow room; it did not work well in the colonial setting, where villages were hemmed in by settlers' farms. Native communities did relocate from time to time – the Mohawks and others living at the mountain moved to Sault au Récollet in 1696, then to Oka in 1721 – but their movements responded more to the pressures exerted by land-hungry habitants than to the needs of the Amerindians themselves.

The Huron refugees who settled in the vicinity of Quebec were even more confined. By the time Peter Kalm visited their village at Lorette, the Hurons had adopted many elements of the French-Canadian agrarian way of life.

When the Jesuits who are now with them arrived among them they lived in their usual huts, which are made like those of the Laplanders. They have since laid aside this custom and built all their houses after the French fashion. In each house are two rooms, *viz.* their bedroom and the kitchen. In one room is a small oven of stone, covered on top with an iron plate. Their beds are near the wall, and they put no other clothes on them than those which they are dressed in. Their other furniture and utensils look equally wretched ...

These Indians have made the French their patterns in several things besides the houses. They all plant corn; and some have small fields of wheat and rye. Some of them keep cows. They plant our common sun-flower (*Helianthus annuus*), in their corn fields and mix the seeds of it into their sagamite or corn soup.

Kalm's impression of this Huron household was of an imperfect and impoverished version of the French rural economy, though in fact his description suggests a synthesis of European and aboriginal elements. (There is wonderful unconscious irony in this European's referring to a native American domesticated plant as 'our sunflower'!) Still, it is clear that the Christian Natives of Canada had great difficulty supporting themselves on the fruits of the soil. Given their completely inadequate land base, it is a wonder they did as well as they did. As it was, the sale of women's craftwork, payments from the government in recognition of the Natives' enormous military contributions, together with some fur-trade earnings, helped to compensate for the shortcomings of their agriculture and to keep the wolf from the door.

3

The Urban Landscape

Four days out of Montreal in August 1749, Peter Kalm's bateau rounded a curve in the St Lawrence, and the Swedish naturalist caught his first sight of the fortifications of Quebec, looming over the rocky heights. Unlike other travellers who would have arrived from the sea by way of the mammoth funnel of the St Lawrence, Kalm was approaching the city through its back door. Even so, Quebec did not fail to impress Kalm with its spectacular setting against a backdrop of mountains. After landing at the docks, he made his way up the narrow, winding road to the upper town – so steep, he marvelled at the drivers of carriages and wagons attempting the descent – and, at the top, he stopped to admire the 'amazing' view from the galleries of the governor's château. Earlier visitors had called this 'the noblest and most extensive Prospect in the World,' with the Île d'Orléans in the distance and the broad St Lawrence, where 'snow white' belugas frolicked over the waves. Right below Kalm were the wharves and the busy streets of Lower Town. 'Most of the merchants live in the lower city, where the houses are built very close together. The streets in it are narrow, very rough, and almost always wet. There is likewise a church and a small marketplace. The upper city is inhabited by people of quality, by several persons belonging to the different offices, by tradesmen and others. In this part are the chief buildings of the town.'

The 'chief buildings' on Peter Kalm's tourist itinerary of the capital were all associated with the government and the Church. The governor and the intendant, the twin heads of the colonial state, each had a substantial 'palace' which served as residence and place of business (the intendant's home even contained courtrooms and prison cells), as well as meeting-place for polite society. 'The governor's wife and the intendant's wife entertain circles as fashionable and witty as you will find anywhere,' pronounced the well-travelled Jesuit Pierre de Charlevoix. In the spirit of the European *ancien régime*, these palaces were also designed to awe the populace with the magnificence of the Bourbons. Kalm noted the presence of a military guard at the entrance to the château. 'When the governor or the bishop comes in or goes out they must present arms and beat the drum.'

This pomp surrounding the governor reflects the fact that he acted as personal representative of the king's majesty for all of French North America. In almost every case a military man and a member of the French *noblesse*, he had command of the colonial armed forces as well as authority to conduct diplomatic relations with Native nations and neighbouring British colonies. Over other aspects of government administration, a governor had to share authority with the colonial intendant. Intendants were normally well-qualified administrators with legal training, financial expertise, and prior experience in the French naval bureaucracy. An intendant was particularly charged with overseeing New France's judicial apparatus and handling the government's accounts; otherwise, he was supposed to cooperate with the governor in administering the colony. Though his office conferred less prestige than that of the governor, a capable intendant could often wield far more real power. Absolutist France provided no outlets for open political debate in Canada, but factional strife of a covert variety, found in many authoritarian regimes, was often intense. Governor and intendant, when they did not see eye to eye, often found themselves at the centre of rival coteries of lower-ranking officials and merchants, each striving to reward his clients with contracts and promotions.

The bishop occupied a third imposing edifice, and under his authority was an assortment of churches and other ecclesiastical institutions: the seminary, the Ursuline convent, the cathedral, the hospital, the Jesuit college, and so on. In strictly numerical terms, the Church certainly outscored the State on Kalm's list of 'chief buildings.' As an institution, it was in fact closely aligned with government as a major component of public power in the colony. Clergy and civil administration worked together to ensure that Canada remained a well-regulated Catholic community. Behaviour that the Church denounced as a sin was often – as in the cases of swearing ('blasphemy') and meat eating during Lent – punished by the courts as a crime. Women convicted of prostitution by the civil authorities would be confided to the nuns to be incarcerated in their hospital and taught to mend their evil ways. In time of war, the convent was transformed into a military hospital. The bishop himself owed his appointment ultimately to the king of France and was expected to sit on the sovereign council as one of the prime actors in colonial politics. This did not prevent him from denouncing immorality in high places, whether it was in the form of fur traders selling alcohol to Natives, society ladies wearing revealing dresses, or officers cheating their soldiers out of their pay. Conflict did occur between priests and governors, but it was the product of divergent tendencies within a partnership joining a French Church and a Catholic State.

Socially and legally, the clergy is best understood as an 'estate,' whose members enjoyed certain privileges recognized by law: among these was exemption from the military and public works that took the place of taxes in New France. Because women could not be ordained, nuns were not, strictly speaking, part of the clergy, but they did partake of the Church's corporate autonomy and special legal status. (For more on the female religious orders, see chapter 4.)

Male priests could be found ministering to the habitants in the rural parishes of the St Lawrence valley and wandering the distant interior in pursuit of Native converts, but it was in the towns of New France where the Church made its presence felt most strongly.

In Quebec, Peter Kalm visited the seminary, with its 'spacious court' and 'large orchard.' He also called at the Jesuit college: much more than a boys' school, this 'magnificently built' edifice functioned as general headquarters for the Jesuits of New France, complete with a church, library, apothecary shop, dining-hall, and accommodation for residents and missionaries who were between postings. At both institutions, boys destined for the priesthood, or the professions and business, learned their Latin, philosophy, and rhetoric. Fees were low and there was always assistance for a few talented children from poor families, but school was not for the masses in New France. Only a minority of the population could sign their names and, in the countryside, fewer than 10 per cent of the habitants could be called literate. As a Protestant, Kalm had a peculiar fascination with nuns, and so he was thrilled to be allowed to visit the Ursulines' convent and the *hôpital-général*, the latter located just outside the walls of Quebec. Not so much a medical institution as was the *hôtel-Dieu*, the *hôpital-général* had more the character of an asylum for the indigent and disabled. Historians who portray the religious orders of New France as 'social welfare' agencies have it only half right: nuns, as well as male friars of the Récollet order, did exercise Christian charity as part of their religious regime, but the aim was not to solve 'social problems.' The accent was on the act of almsgiving and on its spiritual significance to the giver, rather than the needs of the recipient. The religious were not necessarily expected to adjust their hand-outs when times were hard, and they certainly did not aim to eliminate poverty. Accordingly, we find indigent people begging in the streets while widows of military officers occupy comfortable lodgings at the hospital.

Back in the city, Kalm turned his attention to commerce: 'Quebec is the only seaport and trading town in all Canada, and from there all the produce of the country is exported.' His visit happened to coincide with the height of the shipping season: 'When I arrived here I counted thirteen large and small vessels, but in the evening before I left Quebec I counted twenty-three, and they expected more to come in.' The merchants of the capital controlled the colony's legal export and import trade (smuggling between Montreal and Albany, New York, was a different matter) and, though often themselves dependent for credit on French suppliers, they tended to have the upper hand in relations with the inland traders of Montreal. Kalm noted that the Lower Town merchants dressed richly, but he believed they were not as well-off as they 'ought to' have been. The fact is that this man of science, the guest of governors and clerics, was almost totally unacquainted with the colony's merchants and their business practices.

Most enterprises were individual operations, or, at most, limited-term partnerships. If a merchant borrowed capital to import a shipment of wine and the ship was lost at sea, his or her personal fortune sank along with the wine. This is not the way commerce is conducted today, when large corporations dominate the market, and investors stand to lose no more than their initial investment. At the time of New France, only a few giant trading companies created to further State ends were granted the privilege of limited liability, and consequently entrepreneurs had to find other ways to minimize the risks of business. Diversification was the key. Lower Town merchants such as François Havy and Jean Lefebvre normally combined importing, exporting, wholesale, retail, commercial, and industrial operations. These two Norman traders, in partnership at Quebec from 1732 until the eve of the Conquest, brought in cargoes of cloth, salt, wine, and various other French goods, some to be forwarded in bulk to Montreal merchants, some to be sold in their own Lower Town store. To pay for these imports, the partners exported Canadian furs to France, as well as some grain and lumber shipped to the French West Indies by way of Louisbourg. They also operated shipyards which produced vessels for sale in France, as well as a sealing station on the remote coast of Labrador.

Havy and Lefebvre were connected to an informal network linking merchants throughout New France and to the farthest corners of the French Atlantic empire. Traders at Quebec knew one another, and they also knew, personally or by reputation, all the merchants of Montreal and of the major seaports of France and French America; in many cases, they dealt with brothers and cousins strategically scattered around the Atlantic world. Webs of acquaintance helped spread the news about overseas market conditions (through correspondence); they also provided the basis for making decisions about the granting of credit: could merchant x be relied on to pay for this shipment of salt? There was no avoiding such decisions, for in the absence of banks, business could operate only on credit, short-term credit to facilitate payments and long-term credit to raise capital. One could always sue in the case of a default, but then everyone would be a loser as judicial expenses and the claims of other creditors would absorb the lion's share of any assets. Best, then, to grant credit wisely and keep debtors afloat as long as possible. Success in business therefore required shrewd judgment, a knowledge of people, and up-to-date information on market conditions at home and abroad. It also required good relations with government officials, especially during wartime, when fortunes could sometimes be made supplying the king's forces. In peace-time Canada, however, opportunities for enrichment were strictly limited, as compared, for example, with the sugar-rich plantations of the West Indies, and so it is no surprise that business fortunes in the colony were rather modest. Quebec merchants may not have cut as imposing a figure as the highest-ranking members of the Church, the nobility, and the government administration, but they were well represented on the Superior Council and integrated into factions which struggled for control of the colonial state.

Peter Kalm visited Canada in peacetime, but the signs of war were all around him. Montreal, he remarked, 'is pretty well fortified, and surrounded with a high and thick wall,' and Quebec, too, had its wall, though the latter 'was not quite completed when I was there and they were very busy finishing it.' The two towns had always had some sort of defensive works, but towards the middle of the eighteenth century, with tensions mounting between the imperial rivals, France and Britain, hugely expensive fortification projects were pushed to completion in Canada. France supplied the money, but the labour force was composed mainly of local townsmen and habitants, conscripted for a few days a year as part of their militia duty. Walls designed to withstand an artillery assault consisted of massive banks of earth held in place by an outer covering of stone, and it was in the never-ending task of moving earth that the colonial militiamen, together with their carts and horses, made their contribution. Beyond their strictly military function, the walls of Montreal and Quebec served, as was the case in urban Europe at this time, to give the cities definition, sharply separating the town from the straggling roads and crudely built dwellings of the suburbs. They also made it possible for the authorities to regulate the flow of goods to urban markets.

Soldiers were another prominent feature of the urban landscape of New France in 1749. A permanent force of *troupes de la marine* had been set up in the 1680s, with garrisons in Montreal and Quebec and smaller contingents posted to forts in the west. Kalm, whose contact was mainly with the officer corps, thought the men were exceedingly well treated, with bountiful supplies of food, new clothes whenever they needed them, and considerable freedom of movement during peacetime. His comments probably tell us as much about the deplorable situation of the soldiery in most parts of the European world in the eighteenth century as they do about the realities of Canadian military life. Men were recruited primarily in France, and their term of enlistment was, in most cases, unlimited. Every year a few soldiers were discharged on condition that they settle in the colony, and old, disabled, and out-of-commission veterans were often shipped back to France and dumped on the shore to fend for themselves. However, none of the teenagers who entered the colonial forces could count on ever seeing his homeland again. New arrivals, on being inducted into a Canadian company of the *troupes de la marine*, were expected to foot the bill for a drunken initiation party at which they took on a new personal identity, symbolized by a nickname by which they would be known ever after. Many French-Canadian families still carry these *noms de guerre*: Laterreur, Parisien, Lafleur, Provençal, to name but a few.

Military discipline could be brutal, on occasion, but, for much of the time, the men were left unsupervised. Most lived in private homes, billeting being one of the many burdens imposed by the State in lieu of direct taxation on the colonial populace. Soldiers were not allowed to marry without permission, and permission was rarely granted. After deductions, their pay amounted to next to nothing, though they were permitted to take employment when not needed for guard duty or service in the western posts. Indeed, military personnel constituted a vital pool of skilled and unskilled labour, assisting in agriculture, forestry, construction, and various trades. They were paid for their efforts, though often a grasping company commander would skim off a portion of their earnings.

Promotion to the officer corps was unheard of. A great gulf, with national as well as social dimensions, separated the rank and file from the officers. Whereas the former were almost entirely French and lower class, the latter were mostly Canadian-born and noble; and, of course, their salaries and conditions of service were utterly different. Young men entered the officer corps with commissions as cadets or ensigns, obtained through the favour of the governor and normally awarded to officers' sons or nobles (which usually amounted to the same thing). Commissions were not sold, and promotion was mainly by seniority or 'merit.' Historians who speak of the 'significance of the military' in New France certainly have a valid point, but let us remember that 'the military' was anything but an integrated social entity; moreover, its size and importance varied greatly over the years. Through most of the seventeenth century, the military presence was comparatively minor, but when Canada girded for all-out war shortly after Peter Kalm's visit, Montreal and Quebec were overwhelmed with drums, guns, and men in uniform.

Commanding the colonial troops was an officer corps whose membership and that of the male side of the Canadian *noblesse* coincided nicely. The aristocratic nature of the *ancien régime* State revealed itself clearly in the privileges heaped on the noble families of Canada. They received the lion's share of seigneurial grants, as well as officers' commissions, not to mention various gratuities and pensions, as well as lucrative fur-trade licences. Though they comprised only 1 to 3.5 per cent of the population, Charlevoix remarked that 'in New France there are more nobles than in all the other colonies put together,' and that was clearly a problem as far as this eighteenth-century writer was concerned. Louis XIV's France had encouraged the development of a colonial aristocracy, but with aristocratic status devolving on all the sons and daughters of a noble father, the government was soon besieged with hordes of petitioners who all felt entitled to support and preferment. As members of a privileged 'estate' whose distinctive status was recognized in law, nobles were supposed to 'live nobly,' that is, without manual labour or any hint of servility. A business career was therefore highly problematic if it involved serving customers in any way; indeed, commerce was strictly prohibited to French nobles, though their Canadian counterparts were permitted to invest in trade, since that was one of the few means by which they could make substantial money. Seigneurial revenues were generally quite paltry through most of the French regime, and noble families retained their estates mostly for their prestige value and long-term prospects for secure income. For the time being, their material fortunes depended primarily on the military and the State, and consequently noble seigneurs resided mainly in the cities. A stint as post commander in the western interior afforded many an officer the opportunity to make a semi-illicit fortune in the fur trade. While the men of the Canadian *noblesse* pursued their military careers, the women often managed the family finances and estates. Instead of marrying, many daughters took the veil and, as nobles, they generally played a prominent part in the affairs of the colony's religious orders. Though some resided, at least part of the time, on their rural estates, the majority of Canadian nobles were to be found at Quebec or Montreal.

Before setting off for the capital, Kalm had been favourably impressed by Montreal, though it was in every sense a less imposing city than Quebec under the French regime. When he visited, its rapidly growing population had reached only about 3,500, roughly half that of the capital. The country-side was never far away in this little town strung out along the river, with its landmark mountain in the background; Kalm liked to walk out among the 'excellent grain fields, charming meadows and delightful woods.' The religious orders had their hospital, seminary, and other houses, each surrounded by extensive gardens, and a 'castle' was maintained for the governor general's use when he travelled to Montreal to negotiate with visiting Natives. Otherwise, this was a town of modest dwellings. 'Some of the houses in the town are built of stone, but most of them are of timber, though very neatly built.' Since the great fire of 1734, in fact, stone buildings were replacing wooden ones at a rapid rate, and the government required builders to extend side walls well above the roof line as a safety measure to help contain roof fires. Peter Kalm continues: 'Each of the better sort of houses has a seat on each side of it, for amusement and recreation in the morning and evening,' reminding us that, to a degree difficult for modern urbanites to imagine, the streets and squares of this pre-industrial city were a public space of lively social interaction.

'Every Friday is a market day when the country people come to the town with provisions, and those who want them must supply themselves on that day because it is the only market day in the whole week. On that day, too, a number of Indians come to town to sell their goods and buy others.' Quebec's market was held twice a week; there, as in Montreal, grain, meat, and dairy products were offered to buyers; there were also fruits, vegetables, and fish, as well as Iroquois basketry and other handicrafts. The authorities regulated weights and measures and market hours; it also prohibited grain sales outside the market (to head off any attempt to manipulate prices by monopolizing essential food supplies), but otherwise they left buyer and seller free to negotiate a price.

Montreal was the prime staging-ground for the Canadian fur trade. For much of its early history, the little town was indeed the point where Natives exchanged their beaver pelts for knives, axes, combs, blankets, and other European goods. During the 1650s and 1660s, every summer brought hundreds of canoes from the western interior for the annual fur-trade fair. Many of Ville-Marie's early settlers participated in the exchange, and a few became quite wealthy. With time, the fur business settled into a comfortable routine, with French-Canadian canoemen ('voyageurs') tending increasingly to take their wares to Native customers in the distant interior. By Kalm's time, then, Montreal was more a base of fur-trade operations than an actual site of intercultural commerce. Its business community specialized in outfitting expeditions to the west, forwarding pelts to Quebec (or, on the sly, to Albany), and catering to local retail customers. Louise Dechêne's portrait of the Montreal merchants, based, as it is, on a close analysis of estate inventories and account books, reveals none of the frivolity and ostentation Kalm thought characteristic of their class; instead, she finds individuals turning to account the limited opportunities for profit available to them and living the frugal lives that their modest revenues permitted.

Once a contender for fur-trade pre-eminence, Trois-Rivières had been outstripped by Montreal long before Peter Kalm passed it, halfway along his route down to the capital. Though it boasted a regional governor and an Ursuline convent, as well a nearby iron foundry, which made it something of an industrial centre, Trois-Rivières was hardly a major urban centre, even by the reduced standards of New France. Kalm called it 'a little market town which had the appearance of a large village.'

An observant visitor from across the sea, Peter Kalm is, in many respects, an excellent tour guide, but there was much about urban New France that escaped his notice. Some of the sights, sounds, and smells he encountered must have seemed so utterly normal and banal in the context of those times that he would never have thought to remark on them. Only a time-traveller from another century would comment of the absence of street lighting and the fact that night plunged the city into inky darkness, softened only by moonlight, and broken here and there by the illumination spilling through a window from lamps and candles or by a pedestrian's lantern bobbing along the sidewalk. The smell of human waste would have been equally unremarkable. Outhouses were by no means universal, and so the streets of Montreal and Quebec, like those of Stockholm, Helsinki, and Paris, functioned as open sewers, particularly disgusting when spring thaw flushed out a whole winter's accretion. Non-human animals – certainly more numerous in the cities of New France than *homo sapiens* – made their contribution to the mess. Strolling the streets, you would certainly see plenty of horses, as well as dogs pulling small carts (Kalm did note the use of the latter as the 'poor man's horse,' a Canadian peculiarity, he suggests); you might also sense the presence of chickens, cows, and hogs in nearby backyards. Traffic normally moved at a walking pace through the narrow streets, but there were complaints about young officers galloping through town, sending pedestrians diving into snowbanks.

The 'little people' of French Canada, though they formed a majority of the urban population, remain largely invisible in Peter Kalm's account. As a guest of the colonial élite, he had little contact with the artisans, beggars, labourers, prostitutes, soldiers, and market vendors who congregated in the towns of New France, and so he took no notice of them, except for an occasional anecdote about the need to tip the soldiers who rowed his boat from Montreal to avoid being dunked in the river when they arrived at Quebec. Otherwise, the 'lower classes' appear, not as people, but as an aspect of the 'labour shortage': 'A journeyman to an artisan gets three or four livres a day, and a common labouring man gets thirty or forty sols a day. The scarcity of labouring people occasions the wages to be so high; for almost everybody finds it easy to be a farmer in this uncultivated country where he can live well, and at so small an expense that he does not care to work for others.' Viewed strictly from the employer's perspective, this was the essential problem which bedevilled so many colonial administrators, used to the impoverished, low-wage environment of Europe. Historians who point to New France's low population or to the deleterious effects of the fur trade miss the point that was obvious to Kalm and his contemporaries: since colonists had the option of living independently, there was little inclination to work for a master.

Certainly some day labourers could always be found in the towns, as well as in the farming districts of New France. Historians have not so far been able to learn much about them, largely because, as marginal figures, they seldom appear in the documents. Consequently, we do not know whether work as a labourer was mainly a life-cycle experience, an occupation young men pursued for a few years before establishing themselves as habitants or tradesmen, or whether it was more commonly a lifetime's occupation. We do know that day labourers were not numerous: at any given time, they probably accounted for about 10 per cent of Quebec's population. Furthermore, the sources do indicate that this rarity pushed salaries up to the astronomical figures Kalm cites. But even if a man could earn thirty or forty *sols* a day unloading ships or helping a builder excavate a foundation, work essentially ground to a halt in the winter. According to Louise Dechêne's calculations, the average worker, with earnings coming in during only part of the year, would be hard-pressed to maintain himself at even the most basic level over the long run. It was a classic colonial situation: the necessities of life were expensive, opportunities for self-employment were ample, and consequently labour was costly and troublesome.

Faced with just this basic problem, colonizers in other parts of the Americas had recourse to forced labour – enslaved Africans, Native people in bondage, European convicts, and so on – to turn the resources of the New World to account. Similar approaches were tried in Canada as well, but they provided only a partial solution to the 'labour problem.' The French were never strong enough to impose direct labour service on their Native neighbours, and, besides, they found the latter more useful as independent fur trappers and military auxiliaries. They did, however, buy Pawnee prisoners of war from the distant prairies, as well as slaves of African origin (see below, chapter 5), but there was never enough wealth in the colony to support slavery on a massive scale. Employers could also hire indentured workers (*engagés*) or soldiers, two categories of paid, though personally unfree, labour. Only to a very limited extent, then, can one speak of a 'free market' in labour under the French regime, and, where men were free to choose, they generally opted for the independent life of the habitant or the artisan.

It was self-employed craft workers who produced most of the 'goods and services' needed by the inhabitants of New

France. Carpenters and stonemasons built the colony's houses and they received from the owners, not an hourly wage for their time, but a contractually agreed-upon payment for the completed building. Tanners purchased cowhides and used their own vats and chemicals and drying facilities to turn them into leather; the leather they sold to shoemakers, who needed only a little bench and a modest array of awls, needles, and hammers to transform the raw material into finished shoes and boots, made to measure for paying customers. An armourer could repair a gun, or even build one 'from scratch' using wood, brass, and a piece of bar iron. Few of these 'gens de métier' operated entirely on their own: an artisan's shop, like an habitant farm, was normally a family operation. Moreover, some went into partnership, most kept an apprentice, and several hired labourers from time to time. By and large, however, labour was not a commodity abstracted from life and purchased at an hourly rate; instead, work and ownership, conception and execution, remained closely integrated.

There was a looseness to artisanal life in Canada that distinguished it from the heavily regulated world of craft guilds which held sway in pre-Revolutionary France. Here the status of 'master' craftsman was open to anyone who could stake a plausible claim to professional competence; no formal apprenticeship or licence was required. The government did require surgeons to take out a licence, and it subjected butchers and bakers – as custodians of the community food supply – to close supervision, but otherwise anyone could, in theory, offer services to the public. In some of the less-skilled trades, particularly the construction trades, individuals tended to avoid specialization, presenting themselves as a painter one month, a mason the next, and possibly running a hole-in-the-wall tavern on the side. There was greater stability in the more exacting crafts – wigmaking, sculpture, metalwork, for example – and in these apprenticeship was a thriving institution. Not to satisfy legal requirements, but to learn a useful skill, parents confided their boys to a recognized master, typically for a period of three years. The apprentice assisted the master, lived in his home, and ate with his family, and the master was expected to discipline the child, provide for his religious instruction, and impart to him the 'secrets of the art.'

Apprentices, master artisans, soldiers, merchants, priests, and aristocrats: there was an amazing social diversity to these colonial cities, tiny though they were by European standards. And so far, we have made no mention of the 'marginal' elements of urban New France: servants, both free and slave; sailors in port awaiting their next voyage and passing their time with the prostitutes who gathered in the seedy taverns of Lower Town Quebec; market vendors hawking their wares with penetrating voices that disturbed the celebration of Mass in nearby churches; beggars retailing their sad stories from door to door. In a pre-industrial town, all these specimens of humanity lived in close quarters, with very little of the spatial segregation by class which is so characteristic of a modern city. In the crowded streets of Montreal and Quebec, merchants and noble ladies could not avoid contact with stonemasons, soldiers, and prostitutes.

There was no pretense that individuals met as equals in this *ancien régime* society. Artisans doffed their hats when a priest or a government official passed by, and any shop-keeper bold enough to annoy an aristocratic officer over an unpaid bill was liable to be thrashed with a silver-tipped cane as punishment for such 'insolence.' Rank was open and visible, and authority was exercised in the confident knowledge that subordination was ordained by God himself. The government, subscribing to traditional conceptions of the three 'orders' of society, gave preferment to the nobility and the clergy; according to prevailing ideologies, wealth was decidedly not a criterion of rank, though the government did what it could to endow the privileged orders and thus make rank, as far as possible, a criterion of wealth. In the real world, however, money did confer power and influence, with the result that indebted habitants and poor construction workers really did come under the thumb of rich merchants, even though all were 'commoners' and belonged to the same unprivileged order. Assumptions about the proper subordination of women to men, of children to adults, and, in this colonial context, of non-whites to whites, cross-cut the ideology of status orders and the realities of economic class in complex ways, as we shall see in the chapters which follow. It is misleading, then, to think of the society of New France (or any other society, for that matter) as composed of geological strata or rungs on a ladder; inequality was more a matter of *relationships* than of simple position.

The *ancien régime* possessed a language of social inequality, a way of discussing human relations in terms of superiority and inferiority. Superiority (of husband over wife, captain over corporal, noble over habitant ...) normally implied, not just privilege, but also authority, and with authority went responsibility. Superiority was not simply a functional matter; it tended to be seen as a question of intrinsic worth. There were no rigid castes in Canada; even more than in Europe, relations could change, individuals could rise from obscurity to honour. Charles Le Moyne, for example, arrived in Canada as a penniless *engagé*, but he made a killing in the fur trade, purchased a seigneury, and gained admission to the *noblesse*. However, such an ascent was somewhat problematic to the social orthodoxies of the day. Social thinking in the late twentieth century is almost exactly the reverse of this *ancien régime* outlook. We take 'upward social mobility' for granted and only have difficulty with the fact that most individuals do not actually rise to the top. Unlike the hierarchically-minded *ancien régime*, we assume the theoretical equality of every individual, but we are at something of a loss in finding terms to speak of the enormous inequalities of comfort, power, and freedom which actually structure our collective life.

4

Women of New France

Men from Europe who visited New France almost always had something to say about the women of the colony, and their comments were mostly complimentary. Here is a representative example: 'They are witty, which affords them superiority over men in almost all circumstances.' Peter Kalm's journals are chock-full of remarks about the ladies: how they 'dress and powder their hair every day, and put their locks in papers every night,' the way they tease Swedish gentlemen about their awkward use of French, the songs they sing, and so on. By and large, passages such as these from the travel literature are little more than superficial observations on the manners of the upper classes, often spiced with a playful inversion of the 'natural' sexual hierarchy. Bacqueville de La Potherie took some of the shine off his gallantry by revealing his expectations about Canadian women: 'Although they are, in a certain sense, part of a New World, their manners are not as bizarre or as savage as one would imagine. On the contrary, the sex there is as polite as anywhere in the kingdom.' Interesting, though it may be, from a number of points of view, source material of this sort tells us nothing straightforward about the 'position of women' in New France or about how well the realities of that period measured up to modern standards of sexual equality.

French-Canadian women and the men who wrote of their charming 'superiority' all inhabited an early modern world in which it was assumed that woman, because of her nature, needed to be governed by man. Some of our writers were too polite to insist on masculine power in a heavy-handed way, but the ideologues of the period could be startlingly frank when they got down to the fundamental principles of patriarchy. Likening the family to a kingdom, the French political philosopher Jean Bodin wrote of 'the authoritie, power, and commaund that the husband hath over his wife, by the lawes both of God and man: as also the subjection, reverence, and obedience which the woman oweth unto her husband ...' The bishop of Quebec took this same, basically patriarchal, model for granted when he issued advice to colonial wives. A woman owed her husband, not only 'a sincere and cordial love,' but also 'respect, obedience and the sweetness and patience to bear with his faults and his bad moods.' Like other collectivities, the family should operate on the basis of authority and, in this case, it was the paterfamilias who provided that authority, guiding and, if necessary, punishing wife, children, and servants alike. Patriarchy was not a program or a policy consciously devised by power-hungry men; in normal circumstances, it was not a subject for debate and discussion; we should recognize patriarchy as something more profound – a pattern of thinking and acting that had, over the centuries, entered into the customs and into the very languages of Europe, structuring relationships and shaping personal identities.

Most societies build elaborate cultural edifices around the basic male–female polarity, and the Iroquoian peoples who shared the St Lawrence valley with the French had their own construction of gender. There were enough superficial similarities with European ways that the French could recognize some Iroquois practices as 'normal.' Women worked hard taking care of hearth, home, and food, whereas men roamed far and wide; only males could aspire to the prestige attached to success in war; public speaking, a key to political influence, was a male monopoly; and civil chiefs and war chiefs were always men. Yet, in spite of all these shared elements, the Iroquois gender regime stands in basic contrast with that of the French, for it was not patriarchal. Women shouldered the burdens of the domestic economy, but they also enjoyed full control over the household, and a man who did not make himself acceptable to some female-dominated family group would soon go hungry. Descent went through the female line, and therefore only women could bestow the names that men needed when they were elevated to chieftain status. This gave women a preponderant voice in the selection of chiefs. The male monopoly over 'public office' was further offset by the fact that chiefs exercised only very limited powers; among the non-authoritarian Iroquois, command and obedience had nothing to do with the running of villages, tribes, or families. Leaders never made decisions without consulting the wishes of the community and, as members of the community, women made their views known. The Jesuit Joseph-François Lafitau, an astute observer of the Christian Iroquois community of Kahnawaké, was struck by the power of Amerindian women:

Nothing, however, is more real than this superiority of the women. It is of them that the nation really consists; and it is through them that the nobility of the blood, the genealogical tree and the families are perpetuated. All real authority is vested in them. The land, the fields and their harvest all belong to them. They are the souls of the Councils, the arbiters of peace and of war. They have charge of the public treasury. To them are given the slaves. They arrange marriages. The children are their domain, and it is through their blood that the order of succession is transmitted. The men, on the other hand, are entirely isolated ...

With the phrase 'all real authority,' Lafitau shows himself to be the captive of his time and his culture, unable to find terms to describe a society in which no group ruled over another. Others have followed his lead, labelling the Iroquois 'matriarchal,' but the term is misleading, for, although women possessed important powers, they did not rule the community in a general sense. Neither matriarchal nor patriarchal, the Iroquois had a pronounced gender *difference* without a gender *hierarchy*.

Christianity had surprisingly little effect on Iroquois sexual equality. In some of their earliest missionary efforts in Canada, the Jesuits did their best to enforce patriarchal norms, encouraging parents to beat their children, humiliating 'rebellious' wives, and trying to get men to dominate their families. These early attempts to re-engineer Amerindian society met with limited success, however, and the missionaries soon adopted a gentler approach. Among the Iroquois, the most numerous of the Native converts living on the reserves of Canada, the Jesuits found the women more receptive to their religious message than the men, and so they were all the less inclined to promote male rule. To the aboriginal institutions of civic life, the Church added a new set of positions of influence (such as 'dogiques,' or teachers of religion), which, in Kahnawaké at least, were mostly occupied by women. As a consequence, women seem to have enjoyed even greater powers in this Catholic settlement than they did in the old Iroquois homeland.

And what about the white women of French Canada? In their colonial world, as mentioned above, roles were assigned, identities shaped, and conduct judged according to the norms of patriarchy. Recognizing this basic cultural fact takes us only so far in coming to terms with women's actual experience in New France, however. After all, studies in women's history generally indicate that ideals of feminine submissiveness and domesticity tend to leave room for all sorts of divergent behaviour and, even when they mount no overt challenge to male rule, women are often able to carve out female-controlled zones and to fashion for themselves lives of considerable autonomy and dignity. What, then, was the actual condition of women in New France? Were colonial women really in a favoured situation, either as compared with their European counterparts or in relation to Canadian women of later centuries? It depends in part on what is meant by 'favoured' and also on which classes within that enormously diverse category 'women' that one considers.

Our fictional habitant, Marie, had a range of rights, duties, and chores around the house and farm that kept her endlessly busy, but largely autonomous. As a point of contrast, we might consider the leisured existence of Elisabeth Bégon, a lady of the Canadian nobility whose letters are filled with parties, visiting, and political gossip; in the intervals between festivities, boredom was her main enemy. The cooking, the cleaning, and most of the child care in her household would have been done by servants who had precious little of Marie's independence or of Elisabeth's leisure. Servant girls in the city (slaves excepted) were mostly daughters of farm families who were contracted to work at no salary beyond room, board, and a small trousseau, remaining subject to the employer's authority until such time as they married. These three cases illustrate the diversity which makes the concept of a 'position of women' rather elusive. Nevertheless, we can at least examine some of the legal, moral, and physical frameworks that conditioned female existence in the colony and consider the various lives women were able to construct for themselves.

We might begin with a look at marriage, since, for women even more than for men, the marital relationship was of crucial importance. Arranged marriages were almost unheard of and, although upper-class parents sometimes tried to veto a child's choice, young people were normally free to marry whom they pleased. By European standards, women married young, and widows remarried promptly, so that, in early Canada, to be an adult woman was, in the overwhelming majority of cases, to be a wife. Ease in finding a husband and setting up a household might be considered a 'benefit,' given the difficulties attached in this society to the single life, but it was hardly an unmixed blessing. With marriage began a relentless succession of pregnancies and children; for all but the rich, there were also domestic duties to do with preparing meals, sewing, mending and washing garments, cleaning house, tending the garden, and on and on. Then there were those bad moods of the husband which had to be cheerfully endured. Of course, there is no reason to think that complex human relations, like those of a husband and wife, ever conformed exactly to the bishop's simple formula; no doubt many women were forceful in defending their interests within the family. But if a husband dealt violently with a disobedient wife, the law was basically on his side; he was required only to confine himself to 'reasonable correction.'

Giving birth approximately every two years until menopause was the common experience of married women of all classes in the colony. Physicians were not normally involved in parturition unless a serious medical complication arose. Instead, women in labour depended on the assistance of female neighbours and/or a local midwife. In emergencies, a husband or male relative might even officiate. Midwives were usually middle-aged matrons who, through experience and the right sort of reassuring personality, had earned the confidence of their neighbours. In addition to helping the mother, they were also called upon to administer the sacrament of baptism to newborns who seemed in danger of dying (they might even stretch a point and baptize a stillborn), and this religious function made midwives an object of concern for the Church. Local *curés* were supposed to involve themselves in the selection of a parish midwife of unimpeachable moral standing and require her to take a Church-administered oath of office. However, all indications are that it was the women of each rural community who chose a midwife from among their number. The State also involved itself in a small way: towards the end of the French regime, a professionalized corps of trained and licensed midwives was established, though only in the cities of New France. Male doctors began delivering babies after the British conquest and, over the course of a century-long campaign against midwifery, they eventually succeeded in establishing a virtual monopoly in this area. During the

French regime, however, childbirth was still almost entirely under the control of women.

Most Canadian mothers breast-fed their babies, though some urban women relied on wet-nurses. Danielle Gauvreau estimates that about 15 per cent of the babies born in Quebec City in the early eighteenth century were confided to habitant women, mostly in the nearby parish of Charlebourg, to be cared for until age two or three. This practice, later denounced by Rousseau as heartless and unnatural, was quite common in France at the time. There, mothers of the urban élite had recourse to wet-nursing – in part to maintain their social life free from the burdens of infant care and in part because they considered the rural environment healthier – but poor working women also shipped off their babies and, in their case, it was simply because no other child care was available. There was no real equivalent in New France to the impoverished female weavers of Lyon, and so wet-nursing in the colony tended to be for the wives of government officials, military officers, and merchants only; an élite practice, it involved only comparatively small numbers.

Mothers had primary responsibility for the education of young children. After her daughter died, Madame Bégon reverted to the teacher's role in raising her orphaned granddaughter. 'I show her anything she wants to learn: sometimes history of France, sometimes Roman history, geography, rudiments of reading in French and Latin, writing, poetry, stories, any way she likes in order to give her a taste for writing and learning.' Few Canadian mothers would have had the time or the knowledge to offer such an extensive education; the majority would have confined themselves to the catechism, and perhaps a bit of reading. Girls of élite families were schooled in the decorative branches of learning (art, music, foreign languages) by the Ursulines, while more basic instruction was also available in some communities from the Sisters of the Congrégation de Notre-Dame. It is often said that the women of New France were 'better educated' than the men, and it may well be that the mother's duty to impart religious instruction to her children encouraged a larger proportion of women to develop their reading skills. Yet research in the parish registers of the French regime reveals that grooms were always more likely than brides to sign their names. Why the discrepancy? Reading and writing were quite separate skills in this period, reading associated more with religion, writing more with business, and therefore with the male sphere. It would be misleading flatly to assert that women were *more* educated than men, though it is certainly true to say that they were *differently* educated.

Women made an incalculable contribution to the early Canadian economy, 'incalculable' if only because it cannot be measured. While the colonial records make it possible at least to estimate the production of wheat, furs, and other commodities handled mainly by men, we have no idea how much butter, wool, or eggs New France produced. The lack of documentation reflects the fact that activities that were viewed as 'feminine' tended to be seen as subsidiary. Though there was a pronounced gender division of labour at the time, male and female spheres were not yet as radically severed as they would be in later centuries. With the advent of industrial capitalism came the model of the 'breadwinner economy' in which a husband normally worked outside the home and earned a salary, while a wife looked after 'his' home and children and (according to the ideal) remained in the 'unproductive' domestic economy. The split between 'productive' and 'domestic' functions was much less pronounced in pre-industrial societies such as French-regime Canada, where the main economic unit was the family rather than the individual. Since the majority of the population lived in self-sufficient farming households, no one 'brought home the bacon': the bacon (and the bread) were already home. Comparatively few men earned salaries, and most men – from habitants to merchants and high officials – worked, in some sense, 'at home.' Thus, although women's work was devalued, it was not ignored; nor was it viewed as utterly different from the 'real' productive activity performed by men.

The family, rather than the individual, was the main economic actor during the centuries when France ruled Canada, and the family was a team, albeit with unequal members. In addition to taking care of all the usual female areas of responsibility, women frequently contributed directly to the husband's enterprises. It was not considered shocking for a woman to perform tasks identified as male, though men doing 'women's work' risked ridicule. Habitant wives would lend a hand with field work, especially in the harvest season. Urban women married to craftsmen were often a vital part of the operation, at least where retail sales were involved, but even in the actual production. The wives of officers and government officials tended to take an active role in the political manoeuvring that was necessary to a successful career. Some occupations, such as innkeeping, were regarded as proper for either sex.

It was only natural that a widow who had long been involved in the family enterprise might try to continue it after her husband's death. This was particularly the case with commercial operations, so difficult to liquidate, even if one wished to do so. After her husband died, Marie-Anne Barbel ('Veuve Fornel') emerged as one of the colony's foremost traders, with interests in the fur business, brick-making, and real estate. One could list several other female entrepreneurs from the French regime, not all of them widows, and the fact that sex was not a barrier to business success should be noted. However, we should not lose sight of the fact that women entrepreneurs were the exception, not the rule. Nor were they unique to Canada: business women could also be found at this time in Europe and in the British colonies. Laurel Thatcher Ulrich coined the term 'deputy husband' to describe an aspect of the married woman's role in colonial New England. It was considered normal in the seventeenth century for a wife to assume the position of head of household in an emergency or when the man was absent or dead. Were the men of New France more frequently away from home, and the women consequently more likely to take full charge of business, than was the case in other countries? On this point, we really have no solid evidence to go on. It is true that Canadian men were often off on fur-trade expeditions and military operations, but in other countries as well duty called men far from home and hearth.

In one important respect, the economic situation of women in French Canada differed from that in the colonial United States. Marital-property law under the Custom of Paris worked on principles quite dissimilar to those prevalent in places governed by English law. Both the English and the French legal traditions tended to amalgamate the identities of husband and wife when it came to buying, selling, owning, or renting property, but under English law (if we leave aside exceptions and qualifications, for the sake of simplicity), the consolidated identity was that of the husband. William Blackstone, writing about the time of the Conquest of Canada, explained his country's marital regime in these terms: 'By marriage, the husband and wife are one person in law; that is, the very being or legal existence of the woman is suspended during the marriage, or at least is incorporated and consolidated into that of the husband; under whose wing, protection, and cover, she performs everything.' In French Canada, as in the northern half of France, the marital merger did not require a woman to subsume her economic identity under her husband's name. Instead, the couple formed a sort of two-person corporation, the 'marital community' (*communauté de biens*), owned equally by both. Pierre and Marie, the habitant pair we encountered earlier, could be thought of as possessing, each of them, a 50 per cent share in a legal entity called Pierre-and-Marie, and it was this 'person' which owned their land and all their other goods; it could buy or sell, sue or be sued, something neither of them could do as isolated individuals. Consequently, contracts under the civil law of French Canada normally required the signatures of both husband and wife.

This all looks very egalitarian, which it was in a sense, but the marital-community system was not as modern as it sounds. The Custom of Paris states unequivocally that 'the husband is master of the community,' and, when a married woman signed a contract along with her spouse, the notary always recorded the fact that she did so 'with the permission of the said husband.' We should therefore see the *communauté de biens* as conferring on women equal property rights within marriage, but not equal managerial powers. Thus, the day-to-day business affairs of the family were probably run in New France much as they were in, for example, colonial New England: wives were consulted, but men tended to take the lead. It was when one of the spouses died that the special characteristics of French law really came into play. Before the widow or widower could remarry, the old marital community had to be dissolved, and this required an inventory of all the couple's possessions (more wonderful source material for social historians), and a fifty–fifty division of both debts and assets; the survivor retained half, and the rest went to the heirs. If the debts outweighed the assets, a woman could 'renounce the community,' which means that she took away a few personal possessions, then left the rest to the creditors without being required to pay the remaining debts. (A widower had no such privilege; as 'master of the community,' he could not escape responsibility.) In practice, the results obtained after a man died may not have been very different from what occurred in the parts of North America subject to English law, for there men often provided in their wills for a 'widow's portion' to support their wives and for bequests to help their children to get launched in life. In French Canada, however, the outcome did not depend on the man's will (in either sense of the term); married women had an inherent right to a full share of family property, just as daughters could not be deprived of an inheritance equal to that of their brothers.

This legal system survived the Conquest, much to the consternation of British visitors to Canada in the early nineteenth century. 'The wife being by marriage invested with a right to half the husband's property,' one of them wrote, 'and, in being rendered independent of him, is perhaps the remote cause that the fair sex have such influence in France; and in Canada, it is well known, that a great deal of consequence, and even an air of superiority to the husband, is assumed by them.' It was an intolerable infringement on a man's liberty to dispose of his property, the English protested, when he always needed to secure his wife's signature and, since wills had virtually no place in French-Canadian inheritance, a man was not even allowed to decide how his wealth would be distributed after his death. Of course, the indignation stemmed from the unshakable conviction that family property was, or should be, a man's property. Unlike the domestic tyrants found in so many early English novels, a French-Canadian father could not threaten a daughter who fell in love with the wrong man with being 'cut off without a penny,' and he did not have much economic leverage in relation to his wife either. The mechanisms of patriarchy were located elsewhere under the French system.

Although single women were much rarer in New France than in Europe, not every woman became a wife and mother. The religious life did offer one alternative to marriage, an alternative embraced by a small but substantial proportion of the female population – those who entered an order of nuns (about 3.7 per cent of women, according to one estimate). There were no contemplative orders in the colony; instead, they all concentrated on some useful task: the Ursulines had girls' schools, the Augustines de la Miséricorde de Jésus ran the *hôtels-Dieu* of Montreal and Quebec, and the Sisters of Charity of the Hôpital-Général of Quebec administered a general-purpose asylum for the destitute, crippled, and insane. And yet, religious devotion was the central focus of all nuns' lives. A typical day for members of the Hôpital-Général began at 4:30, with an hour's meditation before the holy sacrament; later there was a little time to look after inmates, but at 7:30 the nuns assembled in the chapel to recite the *tierce*, *sexte*, and *none*, followed by mass at 8:00 ... And so the day passed, with individual and collective devotions occupying as much time as tending to the unfortunate. This was as it should be, for nuns were supposed to be women who experienced a special divine calling to take vows of chastity, poverty, and obedience, consecrating their lives to God.

As it happens, they also made a valuable contribution to colonial society with their medical, educational, and social efforts, something which the government recognized and rewarded with annual subsidies. Moreover, they also served other mundane purposes by virtue of their irrevocable commitment to opt out of the processes of biological and economic reproduction. A disproportionate number of nuns came from noble or wealthy families, in part because parents of these classes often found it convenient to place some of their daughters outside the inheritance game. The other reason for the upper-class bias in convent recruitment is that each novice had to pay a substantial 'dowry,' a capital sum intended to ensure the maintenance of the sister, so that the order would not be an economic drain upon the community.

Patriarchal Europe had never been entirely comfortable with the religious communities of women which it harboured. Detached from a family setting and from the authority of husband or father, they lived together in autonomous female collectivities. To contain this potential challenge to gender norms, and equally to ensure the protection of that most precious, but also most fragile of nuns' possessions, their chastity, the Church insisted on *clausura*, the strict confinement of religious women within the cloisters of their convent. The most idealistic women of the Counter-

Reformation, among them Marguerite Bourgeoys of Montreal, chafed at this restriction, for they longed to go out into
the world and do God's work wherever they were needed.
Marguerite, and the Sisters of the Congrégation de Notre-
Dame who followed her, objected to all the trappings of a
regular religious order, including dowries and solemn and
perpetual vows. Avoiding the former kept the Congrégation
open to poor women, while shunning irrevocable vows en-
sured that only the fully committed stayed with the group.
The Sisters did all sorts of pious work in the Montreal area,
assisting the clergy, succouring the afflicted, and instructing
the children. However, they were not unique. Sisterhoods
such as the Congrégation, doing good in defiance of prevailing restrictions on women's religious life, were quite
common in seventeenth-century Europe. The Ursulines, for
example, began in Italy as just such a loose organization
before they were forced to make themselves into something
more like a conventional order of nuns. What made New
France special was the fact that, as a newly founded Catholic
society, it displayed the latest tendencies in Counter-
Reformation idealism without the counterweight of older,
entrenched customs and institutions. Consequently, restrictions such as *clausura* were less rigidly enforced. Still, even
in Canada, the (male) Church hierarchy was unceasing in
its efforts to bring the energies of religious women under
control, and eventually it managed to transform even the
Sisters of the Congrégation de Notre-Dame into something
like a conventional order.

Nuns and quasi-nuns may have constituted only a small
portion of the population, but even for women who married, religion could be an important part of life, one which
opened vistas not otherwise considered part of the feminine
sphere. Devotional confraternities gathered together lay
people for collective prayer and many of them, notably the
most popular, the Confrérie de la Sainte-Famille, came to
be entirely female. These were always under the authority of
the bishop and the parish priest, and the manual distrib-

uted to members stressed the duty of the Christian wife to care for her family and obey her husband. In some respects the Confrérie de la Sainte-Famille can be seen as a manifestation of the Catholic Church's tendency, in the wake of the Reformation, to portray feminine virtue in purely domestic terms. Yet there was still a notion that duty to God came before duty to family, even for a mother. The story was told of Marie Hallé, who left three children under the age of four at home asleep while she went to an early-morning meeting of the Sainte-Famille. She returned home to find them awake, nicely dressed, and waiting patiently; a mysterious lady in white (the Virgin Mary, no doubt) had taken care of them. Now, whereas modern experts in regulating motherhood would have seen this incident as a case of child neglect, the seventeenth-century Church presented it as a miraculous reward for exceptional piety. Clearly the Catholic clergy was somewhat ambivalent, on the one hand telling married women to concentrate on maternal and domestic duties and, on the other, holding up feminine ideals of a very different sort.

And what did the Confrérie de la Sainte-Famille mean to its women members themselves? It is difficult to know for sure, but there are indications that, in addition to its strictly religious purposes, the organization functioned, to some extent, as a women's mutual-aid society. A charitable bequest from Marie Leroy gave the Quebec City Sainte-Famille chapter 'one mattress, one bed frame, two pairs of sheets and six towels ... to be lent to poor women giving birth, asking them to take care of them and return them for the use of others.' Officially dominated by male priests, but operated to a significant degree by women, the Confrérie seems to epitomize the larger situation of women under the patriarchal régime of the period.

In a general sense, men ruled in New France, just as they did in old France. Outside the Iroquois enclaves, where Native women bore heavy burdens but submitted to no one's authority, a basic early modern patriarchy prevailed.

Male power was deeply rooted in the colony's European culture, though not specifically tied to the control of family property, as was the case in the British world. Nor was it as closely connected as it would be in later centuries to a monopoly over professional functions and the breadwinner's income. It was a more diffuse, and at the same time more overt, insistence that women and girls ought to obey husbands and fathers. In Canada and throughout the European world at the time, however, this basic principle of patriarchy left room for all sorts of complexity, diversity, and contradiction in the real-world relations of males and females. There were some particular circumstances of colonial existence – a looseness in the gender division of labour on pioneer farms, the relative importance of uncloistered nuns, and so on – which worked to the advantage of women. Yet, New France was hardly an early modern oasis of equality between the sexes.

5

French and Others

Earlier generations of historians liked to emphasize the homogeneous quality of French Canada's original stock: everyone was from France, they suggested, and everyone was Catholic; racial purity prevailed, and social harmony reigned supreme. New France a homogeneous society? It only looks that way when you ignore the resident Native people, the African slaves, the English-American prisoners, the French Protestants, and the other minorities who lived there; and that is, of course, exactly what these conservative nationalist historians did. Certainly it is true to say that French Catholics predominated in the colony, but they were not alone; nor were they unaffected by the minority groups. When we take proper notice of all the people who were not Catholic, not French, or not white, it becomes apparent that New France was, in fact, a multicultural society.

Relations between Europeans and Natives were, of course, crucial to the history of colonial Canada. It is often said that the French were unique among the European nations colonizing the Americas in their ability to get along with aboriginal peoples, and there is certainly some truth to this observation. The Spanish and Portuguese built empires on conquest and subjugation, reducing the Indians of South and Central America to various forms of servitude. But the more loosely organized societies of Canada were not as conquerable as the Native civilizations of Mexico and Peru, and the French were, in any case, not strong enough to impose a heavy yoke. Thus there was no tribute in New France, no labour-service obligation, and enslavement affected only the distant Pawnees. More characteristic of the British pattern of colonization in the future United States was a bitter conflict over land, one in which Indians were massacred, marginalized, or exiled from their homelands. Such conflict was not completely absent from Native–French relations, but it was far less prevalent, simply because the French-Canadian population was small and concentrated in a limited area not heavily occupied by Amerindians.

The French may have inflicted less immediate damage on aboriginal America than did the Spanish, the English, and the Portuguese, but, in their own way, they were no less imperialist than the others. They did not hesitate to claim sovereignty over gigantic tracts of North American territory without even pretending to purchase them from the original inhabitants. Moreover, they did tend to see Natives as, at best, useful resources. What the French of Canada wanted from their neighbours was, not so much their land or their servile labour, but their furs and, after the 1680s, their powerful assistance in war. Effective military allies and fur suppliers had to have space and autonomy, so that it was in the French interest to develop a comparatively subtle version of colonialism.

French-Canadian settlers of the St Lawrence valley had contact with two different categories of Amerindians: the permanent residents of the Christian reserves located right in the midst of the colony, and the distant nations of the '*pays d'en haut*,' the vast inland territories claimed by the king of France but never effectively occupied by his subjects. The more numerous peoples of the second category were tied to the French, more or less firmly, by commercial and diplomatic links which required constant reaffirmation and frequent voyages back and forth along the canoe routes of the Great Lakes and the Ottawa River. In the second half of the seventeenth century especially, every summer brought hundreds of Ojibway, Illinois, Ottawa, and other Natives to the gates of Montreal. They came from Georgian Bay, the Upper Mississippi, Lake Superior, and beyond, and their aim was, apart from experiencing the adventure of the voyage, to trade for European goods and to confirm their alliance with the French. 'They begin to arrive in large bands in the month of June,' writes Bacqueville de La Potherie. 'The chiefs of each nation first go to greet the governor to whom they present some pelts, asking him to ensure that they are not overcharged for their purchases ... They hold a fair along the edge of the river...' The colonial governor would usually travel up from Quebec for the occasion, and, in his fatherly role as 'Onontio,' he would distribute presents to his 'children' and try to arbitrate any disputes troubling the alliance system.

Some version of the Montreal fair continued to the end of the French regime, but the main point of contact in the fur trade moved farther to the west as travelling French-Canadian traders, the 'coureurs de bois,' took their wares to Native customers in the interior. These young men soon learned the ways of the birchbark canoe, mastered Native languages, established liaisons with aboriginal women, and generally adopted large elements of Amerindian culture. They maintained a tenuous contact with the St Lawrence settlements, where Church and State tended for many years to regard them as dangerous renegades. At the same time, their situation on the cultural borderlines obviously made them highly useful to the government, particularly in times of war, and so they were never complete outcasts. Over the course of the eighteenth century, the previously chaotic fur trade was rationalized along capitalist lines, and wage-earning canoemen (confusingly referred to as 'engagés' even though they were not in the same position as the transatlantic labourers of the previous century) became more common than independent traders. Like the *coureur de bois,* the *engagé* adopted many elements of the Native way of life; he was, however, a worker, subject to the discipline of a master.

Young men voluntarily immersing themselves in a Native environment, the *coureurs de bois* and the *engagés* had their counterparts in the other settler populations of the New World: the *bandeirantes* of Brazil, the *vaqueros* of Spanish America, the frontiersmen of the future United States. Yet this sort of movement back and forth and along the intercultural frontier zone does seem to have been more prevalent among the Canadian French. The circumstances mentioned earlier doubtless go a long way towards explaining their success in this area (though that cannot be the whole story: the French also got along rather well with the Tupi of Brazil and the Caribs of the West Indies). That being said, it is important not to romanticise the relationship or to overlook its manipulative aspects. Even the *coureur de bois* Nicolas Perrot, who sometimes seemed more Native than European after all his years in the *pays d'en haut,* tended to speak of Indians, not as equal partners with the French, but as difficult inferiors who need to be 'managed' lest they 'stray from their duty.'

Meanwhile, as exchanges continued between French Canada and the aboriginal *pays d'en haut,* Native communities continued year-round in the midst of the Laurentian colony itself. The most important of these were the two predominantly Iroquois settlements, Kahnawaké and Oka (Kanesataké), near Montreal, and the mainly Huron village of Lorette near Quebec. All were officially known as 'missions,' and each was under the auspices of a religious order (the Jesuits in most cases), and certainly an Iroquoian version of Christianity was an important part of the identity of these communities, but that does not mean that they were fully controlled by the priests. The mission Indians were, in fact, largely self-governing, economically independent, culturally autonomous, and, as such, their situation stands in striking contrast to that of South American Natives then under the control of European missionaries. The Guarani of Paraguay, to take one famous example, were forced by the Jesuits to wear a sort of uniform, to labour in plantation fields, and to submit to flogging for disobedience and 'laziness.' Iroquoian converts in Canada, though they accorded an influential place to their European missionaries, would not dream of putting up with that sort of treatment.

The Kahnawaké Mohawks not only rejected clerical tyranny, but explicitly refused to acknowledge the sovereignty of the king of France. Their conception of sovereignty was ethnic rather than territorial, and so, while they viewed the governor of New France as a 'father,' they did not consider themselves bound by French law, even in the middle of His Majesty's Canadian settlement. Eventually, the colonial government came tacitly to accept Iroquois autonomy and it gave up trying to prosecute Natives for criminal offences. It also turned a blind eye to trade with the English, trade which was considered contraband when carried on by French Canadians. The colonial state's capitulation was dictated mainly by military prudence, for, in wars with the unconverted Iroquois League, and later with the English, the mission Indians were a central element in the defence of New France.

What about the Jesuits? Did they tolerate aboriginal ways out of some liberal 'cultural relativism' centuries ahead of their time? Not really. Even though they found much to praise in the customs of the Canadian 'sauvages' (fortitude, patience, generosity ...), the Jesuits still tended to see Native culture as fundamentally an affront to God's law, and this attitude pervades their writings. In so far as they tolerated Native ways, they did so largely because they had no choice. One missionary toiling fruitlessly in the far west expressed his frustration in these revealing terms. 'Nothing is more difficult than the conversion of these Savages; it is a miracle of the Lord's mercy: we must first make men of them, and afterward work to make them Christians. As they are absolute masters of themselves without being subjected to any Law, the independence in which they live enslaves them to the most brutal passions.' If independence is what 'enslaves' unconverted Natives, presumably subjection to Jesuit rule is what they need.

In the first half of the seventeenth century, the newly arrived French Jesuits had indeed tried to introduce a highly disciplined mission system, consciously modelled on the Paraguayan *reducciones*. At Sillery, they gathered together some vulnerable Montagnais and Algonguins, already weakened by war and famine, and tried to regulate everything from hunting activities to marital relations, with the whip and the jail cell at hand for stubborn sinners. Not surprisingly, the experiment proved a failure, since Natives naturally steered clear of that sort of sanctified concentration camp. Eventually, the astute and resourceful Jesuits developed a gentler, less obtrusive mission regime, one which worked much more successfully in the Canadian setting. The broader context of Native–European power relations forced them to take this more accommodating approach. Their colleagues in South America could take a much more exacting line because the Natives they ministered to were already exposed to the oppression of white conquerors. The Guarani were not constitutionally more submissive than the Iroquois, but the alternative to accepting the regulated life of the Paraguayan *reduccion* was to place oneself at the mercy of ferocious slavers and ruthless *encomenderos*, whereas Natives outside a Canadian mission faced no such perils. Like the colonial state, the missionary Church in New France had to tread carefully or 'their' Natives would simply leave. Because they had to adapt to Indian ways in order to maintain their influence, the Canadian Jesuits came to have – almost in spite of themselves – a good appreciation of Native cultures. Some, such as Father F.-J. Lafitau, often hailed as a pioneer of comparative ethnography, wrote knowledgeably and sympathetically of aboriginal customs and beliefs. However, the contrast with the Latin American experience should teach us that this broad-mindedness was the product of a peculiar balance of power, not of any pre-existing 'liberal' mind-set on the part of the Jesuits.

The Jesuits did their best to minimize unregulated contacts between Native converts and French settlers, a policy which, for a time, brought them into conflict with the colonial government. In the 1660s and 1670s, the administration in France and its officials in Canada proclaimed the need to Frenchify the mission Indians, to bring settlers and Natives together 'to constitute one people and one race.' French men were to marry Native women, white families were to adopt Indian children, and the result would be a strengthened French colony. The results proved disappointing. There were intercultural adoptions, but not always in the direction favoured by the bureaucrats; eventually more French-Canadian orphans and bastards were placed with Native families than Indian children with French parents. And, as for marriage, the barriers of language and custom worked to keep the races apart. Certainly there was some intermarriage, but it was not nearly as prevalent in the Laurentian heartland as in the *pays d'en haut*, where *coureurs de bois* adapted to Native ways and married Native women. For a number of very good reasons, assimilation did not work, but officials such as Governor Frontenac saw only the stubborn refusal of the Jesuits to 'civilize' the Indians.

At one level, this was simply a conflict of imperialist ideology versus imperialist experience. The ideology, common among European explorers, newly arrived missionaries, and the monarchs who sent them, from the time of Columbus until after the end of New France, assumed that 'savages' were culturally deficient humans who ought to recognize the obvious value of European tutelage. The results of assimilation and intermarriage would be an amalgamated people which would naturally follow European norms. In this world-view, savagery was the negation of civilization; uncivilized Indians did not have a *different* culture, they had *no* culture. They had no religion, only a collection of weird delusions; no government, no authority, no manners; no proper language, only strange babbling noises. Converting them to Christianity and assimilating them into European society (at a subordinate level, of course) should be a matter merely of filling a void. Since this one-culture outlook had no place for a fully developed, but different, way of life, it led inevitably to frustration, since Indians never did, and never could, play their assigned part. In Latin America, this frustration sometimes led to sadistic tendencies, as conquerors lashed out against the 'ungrateful' and 'stubborn' Natives, but in Canada the response was more muted, and much of the resentment was channelled towards the Jesuits rather than the Amerindians. The Jesuits, for their part, never really rejected the one-culture model, but they applied it with far greater sophistication than the uninformed colonial administrators. Long and dedicated missionary experience taught the Jesuits about the reality, the complexity, and the tenacity of Amerindian culture; it never convinced them that the aboriginal way of life was anything but evil.

From today's vantage point, it is striking to note how small a part 'race,' in the modern sense of the term, played in these discussions. If your view of imperialism is oriented towards late-nineteenth-century biological racism, with its notion of the 'white man's burden' and the innate inferiority of the 'coloured races,' then it may be a surprise to learn that this seventeenth-century colonial regime favoured racial amalgamation. In fact, Europeans of this period did not attach overriding significance to skin colour or other visible characteristics of racial difference. Nor did they generally believe that one section of humanity was born with greater capabilities than others. People were potentially equal, but they did not all live according to the same rules – some of them failed to follow God's law and some of them refused to live in a civilized manner.

The debate between the 'assimilationist' project of the government and the 'segregationist' tendencies of the Jesuits faded out over the decade of the 1680s. The reason: war, first with the unconverted Iroquois League, and then with the English. From then on, the government valued the mission Indians primarily as fighting forces, and the idea of dissolving them into the settler population could not have been further from its mind. The Jesuits demonstrated their allegiance to His Majesty by encouraging Native military efforts and, by and large, missionaries and governors pursued their aims in a cooperative spirit.

The authorities' anxieties about assimilation came to be focused more on the French Canadians than on the Amerindians. Some Europeans, war captives and others, did cross over entirely into aboriginal societies. More numerous were those who, like the *coureurs de bois*, frequented the western interior and adopted a quasi-Native identity. 'Mainstream' French-Canadian society also picked up elements of Native culture, and these did not escape the notice of Peter Kalm.

Though many nations imitate the French customs, I observed, on the contrary, that the French in Canada in many respects follow the customs of the Indians, with whom they have constant relations. They use the tobacco pipes, shoes, garters, and belts of the Indians. They follow the Indian way of waging war exactly; they mix the same things with tobacco; they make use of the Indian bark boats and row them in the Indian way; they wrap a square piece of cloth round their feet, instead of stockings, and have adopted many other Indian fashions.

This summer visitor might also have mentioned snowshoes, as well as the Native remedies and therapeutic techniques which worked their way into settler medicine.

These important contributions to the emergent colonial way of life tended to go unnoticed or undervalued by the French élite, who tended to be preoccupied with something more sinister borrowed from the Indians by Canadian settlers: freedom. Father Charlevoix voiced it thus: 'I could

not, Monseigneur, adequately express to you the attraction
which the young men feel to this savage way of life which
consists of doing nothing, in being restrained by nothing, in
pursuing all one's urges, and placing oneself beyond the
possibility of correction.' Charlevoix was referring specifically to the *coureurs de bois*, but he had in mind a more
pervasive aboriginal influence which he and other com-
mentators felt was corroding relations of authority and subordination generally. Proximity to 'savages' – when added
to the effects of living in a raw and savage land – explained
why Canadian parents were too lenient, children too independent, wives too domineering, workers too demanding.
In Charlevoix's moral universe, savagery – basically, the
absence of restraint – was a dangerous contagion, always
threatening to undermine the health of civilization. Historians are sometimes too quick to take statements such as his as
factual descriptions of the effects of the Native presence on
French-Canadian settlers, when, in fact, they are nothing of
the kind. The latter may well have learned something about
liberty from their Indian neighbours, but we have seen in
earlier chapters that they had other reasons, rooted in such
factors as the abundance of land, to act somewhat differently than Europeans. Charlevoix and other writers and
administrators of his class use phrases such as 'the savage
way of life' to express their anxieties about order and authority and the difficulties of preserving them in a colonial
setting. Even slavery, the ultimate relationship of subordination, to which we now turn, carried no guarantee against
the danger of chaos.

Montreal in 1734: two terrible fires broke out that year –
though only one involved loss of life – and, like burning
torches, they both shed light on the difficult issue of race
relations under the French regime. The first blaze occurred
on the evening of 10 April, when a black slave, Marie-
Joseph-Angélique by name, deliberately set fire to her
mistress's house near the riverside. A strong west wind
spread the conflagration, and within three hours, forty-six

buildings had been destroyed, though no one seems to have been seriously injured. Some months earlier, Angélique had run away, accompanied by a French-Canadian servant from the same household, Claude Thibault, who was probably her lover. In two weeks on the loose, the pair failed to find their way to New England and they were captured by the authorities; Thibault went to jail for a time, and Angélique simply went back to her duties. She did not get along with her mistress, Madame de Francheville, and was often scolded and 'mistreated' (beaten). Her main complaint seems to have involved another maid in the Francheville household; Angélique could not stand this white woman and asked the mistress to get rid of her. Madame de Francheville complied. Slave and slaveowner continued to quarrel, however, and, after the abortive escape, it was resolved that Angélique would be sold to a West India plantation as soon as navigation opened in the spring. With this dreadful prospect in view, the black woman turned to arson in a desperate act of pre-emptive vengeance.

They picked her up the next morning, sleeping in the yard of the burnt-out hospital, and soon her trial began. The surviving portions of the testimony make it clear that the court was working on the assumption that hers was the crime of a cantankerous servant irritated by trivial personal grievances. The judges took little notice of witnesses who testified that Angélique railed against the French, dreamed of going back to her country (Portugal or Portuguese Africa), and threatened to kill her mistress if she did not give her a 'congé,' the discharge by which soldiers or *engagés* were released from service. An indentured servant could look forward to a *congé*, a slave could not; and, though she had a natural tendency to personalize her grievances, it was ultimately slavery itself that kindled Angélique's fury.

No one knows exactly how many slaves there were in Canada at this time; there were probably several hundred in Montreal, the major slaveholding centre in the colony. Almost all were, like Angélique, employed as domestic ser-

vants. Slavery was a central element in the European colonization of the Americas, and so white settlers considered the
institution perfectly normal, even though the economy of
New France had room for only a limited number of slaves.
No shiploads of human chattels were ever imported directly
from Africa, though slaves of African origin did enter Canada
in small numbers as war booty or through casual trade with
the Caribbean and the British colonies. More numerous
were 'panis' servants, Native people (mostly Pawnees) purchased from the far west. The presence of the latter in
eighteenth-century Montreal reflected economic connections between that city and the French settlements on the
Mississippi. A *panisse* named Marie worked in the house
next door to Madame de Francheville's, and she and
Angélique seem to have been good friends, constantly visiting each other's kitchens to borrow a fish or to share a joke.

Testimony at Angélique's trial reveals much about the
conditions of early Canadian slavery. Through this unusual
documentary window, we see Angélique supervising
neighbourhood children at play, wandering the town in
search of dandelion greens for salad, chatting with a soldier
on guard duty, sharing impromptu sports with Marie. Clearly
she enjoyed considerable autonomy in her day-to-day duties. Her life was nevertheless hard. She had no bedroom of
any sort, but slept instead on a pallet on some corner of the
floor; her meals were basic; and she had to endure her
mistress's intermittent disciplinary outbursts. But then, the
free white servants with whom she lived and worked seem to
have been no better off. Images of slavery derived from the
nineteenth-century American South are unhelpful when we
wish to understand this earlier form of servitude. In New
France, there was no simple dichotomy with free and white,
on one side, unfree and black, on the other. Instead, there
were degrees and varieties of unfreedom, with many French
people (servants, *engagés*, apprentices, soldiers) subject to
the authority of a master in almost the same way that a slave
was. At this level of society, barriers of race and legal status

were minimal. Thus, close relations – marked by love, hate, friendship – between a black slave such as Angélique and the white people around her were not out of the question.

Does this mean that Canadian slavery was benign or, as one historian puts it, 'familial'? Not when the family of which the slave was a marginal member was never her own family. Northern slaves may have been spared the rigours of plantation gang labour, but they also missed even the limited opportunities available to slaves in tropical colonies to enjoy sex, children and family life. Slavery also entailed a diminished personal identity more severe than that inflicted on subordinate whites. Marie-Joseph-Angélique and her friend Marie had no last names: in the records they are simply 'la négresse' and 'la panise.' Marie apparently knew how to sign her name, something most of her free contemporaries in the colony would have been incapable of, but, in a sad irony characteristic of the period, she initially hesitated to sign the legal documents, thinking that she needed to write her master's name: after all, she was taught to think of herself as nothing more than 'the panise of Sieur Bérey.'

Two months after the great fire of 1734, Angélique was condemned to death. The Superior Council – the colony's court of appeal – was certain that she had put the torch to Madame de Francheville's house, but it was equally sure that a mere 'négresse' could not have committed such an audacious act entirely on her own. Accordingly, they ordered her put to the 'question extraordinaire,' interrogation under torture, hoping they could force her to implicate Claude Thibault. They were disappointed, however, for she withstood the pain without cracking. That ordeal past, it was decided to mitigate the original sentence of burning at the stake, and so a merciful executioner hanged her first before consigning her dead body to the flames.

Complex and even intimate, the relationships of early Canadian slavery were nevertheless founded upon an underlying brutality which comes to the surface in the story of Angélique. Another form of brutality, the brutality of war, brought to New France hundreds of civilian captives and military prisoners from the English colonies. This version of the Other in bondage was a significant presence during the war years of the early 1700s, as well as the 1740s and 1750s. In the grim days of the Seven Years War, British and British American prisoners were jammed into the disease-infested prisons at Quebec or hired out to private parties and put to work in the town or in the fields until such time as they might, if they were lucky, return home in a prisoner exchange.

More poignant are the stories of civilian captives – men, women, children – carried off from the frontiers of New England by raiding parties from Canada. Most expeditions were composed of some combination of Canadian militia, *troupes de la marine*, and mission Indians; the last were usually in the majority and, for Natives, the taking of captives was a central part of warfare. Prisoners who survived the arduous march north would usually be ransomed and returned to their homes sooner or later, in many cases much later. Those taken by Indians were sometimes purchased by French officers on their arrival, and then held in the colony pending reimbursement. Many Canadians, moved by the plight of captured enemy civilians, made great sacrifices to rescue them from the Native allies, but the effect of such humanitarianism, coupled, as it was, with support for frontier raids, was to encourage the mission Indians to think of American settlers as so much merchantable booty. Even so, many captives were taken, in keeping with aboriginal custom, to live in an Iroquois or Abenaki community. Christian Indians did not normally kill, or even harm, prisoners at this stage, a departure from earlier Iroquoian custom, but they did sometimes treat them as menial servants. If they were not ransomed, these prisoners were usually integrated into their captors' kinship system.

Though most captives made their way home eventually, many, particularly the young, actually chose to remain in Canada. Historian John Demos has immortalized Eunice

Williams, the daughter of the Puritan minister of Deerfield, Massachusetts. Carried off in 1703, at the age of nine, to Kahnawaké, she broke her poor father's heart, first by converting to the religion of Rome, later by marrying a Mohawk 'savage' and refusing to return to New England. There were many other similar cases. Mostly they involved children, and usually marriage or religious conversion was the crucial step dividing the captive from his or her country of origin. Some were assimilated to the French-Canadian, rather than the Native, population. Those entrusted to the care of the nuns often found the combination of kindness and relentless pressure to abjure heresy irresistible. Some American girls even became nuns, among them Esther Wheelwright of Wells, Maine, who ended up Mother Superior of the Ursulines of Quebec.

Anglo-Americans were not the only Protestants subjected to the nuns' special treatment of smiles, prayers, exhortations, and beverages secretly laced with pulverized saints' bones. Huguenot soldiers or sailors from France who happened to fall ill in Quebec were likely to find that this was part of their hospital regime. There were not really supposed to be any Protestants resident in New France, but, in fact, they were never entirely absent from the colony. Quebec traded extensively with the port of La Rochelle, long a Protestant stronghold, and many of the merchants of Lower Town were Huguenots with La Rochelle connections. Because they played a vital role in colonial commerce, the government accorded them some degree of toleration as long as they did not celebrate their religion publicly. Louis XIV's crackdown on heresy after 1685 made life even more difficult for New France's religious minority, but by keeping a low profile they managed to retain a narrow space for themselves until the end of the French regime.

'Multicultural' is the modern term that best captures a fundamental feature of early Canada's make-up. That there was a French Catholic ascendancy is undeniable; in the official Bourbon vision of colonial development, only a single cultural identity was fully recognized. Protestants were to be present only temporarily, as prisoners awaiting repatriation or as businessmen in transit. Natives, from this same perspective, were in a state of suspension, their humanity not fully realized since they had not yet been subsumed, absorbed, and digested into the Christian culture of Europe. As for the black and Native slaves of New France, they were theoretically pieces of property rather than members of a civil society. It is important to recognize this dominant view of the period, but we are not required to perpetuate it in our retrospective study of French-regime society. Although those who set the tone, gave the orders, and wrote the documents in the seventeenth and eighteenth centuries refused to recognize the distinctive identities of cultural minorities, the latter did exist. A real and enduring presence in New France, non-Catholic, non-white elements formed an indispensable and influential part of colonial society.

6

Beyond Canada

Having looked closely at the colonial society that grew up in the valley of the St Lawrence – 'Canada,' in the older, narrow sense – it is time to turn to the that larger New France which lay beyond, small and scattered French settlements stretching over half a continent. First in order of seniority come the maritime colonies of what is now Atlantic Canada. Founded as offshoots of the centuries-old French cod fishery, Acadia, and then Île Royale, guarded the eastern approaches to the St Lawrence. An inland appendage to Canada took shape in the second half of the seventeenth century, when fur traders and missionaries established a French presence in the Great Lakes region. Finally, with the founding of Louisiana in the early 1700s, the Mississippi valley and the Gulf of Mexico were colonized.

The colony that the French called 'l'Acadie' (Acadia) in the seventeenth century was essentially the land of the Mi'kmaq in what is now Nova Scotia and adjacent parts of the Maritime provinces. By the time the French came to settle among them (1604), the Mi'kmaq had had almost a century of regular contact with Europeans of various nations, mostly fishermen, but also, of late, seagoing fur traders. A Jesuit missionary estimated their population in 1611 at between 3,000 and 3,500, far below its level in earlier generations. 'They are astonished,' Father Pierre Biard added, 'and often complain that, since the French mingle with and carry on trade with them, they are dying fast and the population is thinning out. For they assert that, before this association and intercourse, all their countries were very populous and they tell how one by one the different coasts, according as they have begun to traffic with us have been more reduced by disease.' The Mi'kmaq nevertheless welcomed the French and went to great lengths to assist the first settlers of Port Royal.

The Mi'kmaq were an Algonquian people who drew their living from fishing, hunting, and gathering. The bounty of the sea and of the land was seasonal, and therefore at frequent intervals the Mi'kmaq had to pack their belongings into their birchbark canoes and move on. 'From the month of May up to the middle of September, they are free from all anxiety about their food; for the cod are upon the coast, and all kinds of fish and shellfish ...' In September, many bands went to interior streams to catch eels. Smaller groups would break off in the late fall and winter to hunt for moose, beaver, caribou, and other animals. With the summer, most Mi'kmaq returned once again to the coast. To many Europeans of the time, 'wandering nomads' such as the Mi'kmaq exemplified the instability characteristic of 'savages,' but in fact their movements were anything but aimless; rather they were part of an intricately organized strategy for harvesting food resources and other necessities of life where and when they occurred. Whereas Europeans had long bent their efforts to forcing the land to yield a year-round subsistence in a particular place, the Mi'kmaq and other similar societies concentrated on the technology of mobility and adaptation. Their canoes, snowshoes, and toboggans were a wonder to the French. 'The Savages of Port Royal can go to Kebec in ten or twelve days by means of the rivers, which they navigate almost up to their sources; and thence, carrying their little bark canoes for some distance through the woods, they reach another stream which flows into the river of Canada [St Lawrence], and thus greatly expedite their long voyages.'

In the midst of the Mi'kmaq, a French settler society took root in the seventeenth century and developed a unique way of life, quite distinct from that of Canada. Small in number and on the periphery of empire, the Acadians carved out farming communities for themselves in isolated niches around the Bay of Fundy. Though they eventually outnumbered the aboriginals, these whites generally enjoyed good relations with the Mi'kmaq, in part because they intruded only minimally on the Native resource base. The Mi'kmaq felt more serious pressure from northern New England and, through most of the first half of the eighteenth century, they were locked in deadly combat with the English; frequently the French Acadians were their comrades-in-arms.

War and imperial competition shaped the fates of Mi'kmaq and Acadians in fundamental ways. An out-of-the-way corner in many respects, Acadia had what turned out to be a strategic location when France and England came to blows, for it could be regarded either from the British perspective as New England's northern outpost or, from the French point of view, as the eastern bulwark of Canada. With its long, exposed coastline, Acadia was vulnerable to seaborne raids and invasions; indeed, the colony's seventeenth-century history is punctuated by several interludes during which the English captured and held the infant settlement. In 1713, it was formally ceded to Britain and has since been known as the province of Nova Scotia. However, the settler population remained Acadian French, with a problematic relationship to the crown of England until 1755. Then, during a tense phase of the Seven Years War, the military authorities declared the Acadians a security risk and ordered a mass deportation. The ensuing 'grand dérangement,' the central cataclysm of Acadian history and popular consciousness, saw people shipped off to different ports on the coast of the Thirteen Colonies. This turned out to be only the beginning of a decades-long odyssey which saw survivors making their way via France, Canada, and the West Indies to new homes in Louisiana, Nova Scotia, New Brunswick, and other havens.

The Acadian settlements were in their prime from about the 1670s until the expulsion, and, during that period, the Acadians prospered and multiplied. Beginning with only a few hundred immigrants, the white population grew even more rapidly than that of Canada. By 1710 there were almost 2,000 Acadians and, fifty years later, there were about 10,000. By all accounts, the Acadians had a secure and ample food supply and, with their dispersed rural habitat, they escaped epidemics and lived remarkably healthy lives. By the late seventeenth century, the original Acadian settlement at Port-Royal, near the mouth of the Annapolis River, had spawned new communities at Beaubassin and around the Minas Basin at the head of the Bay of Fundy. Though they traded with the Mi'kmaq, New Englanders, and French, these little communities tended to be rather isolated and self-contained. Local women married local men, with the result that, in the parish of Grand-Pré between 1727 and 1755, 44 per cent of marriages required dispensations for consanguinity (i.e., permission to marry someone officially considered a 'relative' by the Catholic Church).

Though they never strayed far from salt water, the Acadians had little to do with the fishery; their livelihood came from farming. And they created their fields, not by felling forests, but by draining the extensive and nutrient-rich marshes dotted around the Bay of Fundy. The sieur de Dièreville, a French merchant who stayed in the colony for a time (1699), described the unique Acadian approach to agricultural pioneering:

To grow Wheat, the Marshes which are inundated by the Sea at high Tide, must be drained; these are called Lowlands, & they are quite good, but what labour is needed to make them fit for cultivation! The ebb & flow of the Sea cannot easily be stopped, but the Acadians succeed in doing so by means of great Dykes ... Five or six rows of large logs are driven whole into the ground at the points where the Tide enters the Marsh & between each row, other logs are laid, one on top of the other, & all the spaces between them are so carefully filled with well-pounded clay, that the water can no longer get through. In the centre of this construction, a Sluice is contrived in such a manner that the water on the Marshes flows out of its own accord, while that of the Sea is prevented from coming in. An undertaking of this nature, which can only be carried on at certain Seasons when the Tides do not rise so high, costs a great deal, & takes many days, but the abundant crop that is harvested in the second year, after the soil has been washed by Rain water compensates, for all the expense. As these Lands are owned by several Men, the work upon them is done in common ...

Dyke maintenance was a burden, but the fertility of the soil was inexhaustible. Besides growing wheat, the Acadians raised cattle, for their own food and, after 1720, as an export commodity. 'They have an abundance of every kind of vegetable,' Dièreville enthused, '& all are excellent. There are fields of white-headed Cabbage & Turnips ... Nourishing soups are made of them, with a large slice of Pork.' This visitor savoured the wildfowl of the Bay of Fundy, the locally produced maple sugar, the various fruits, wild and domestic; a connoisseur from Normandy, he even approved of the colonial apples.

There were no direct taxes in Acadia and only intermittent collection of tithes. The land was theoretically subject to seigneurial tenure, but rents were seldom exacted and seigneurialism remained a dead issue. There were really no cities in Acadia, only a cluster of shops and houses around the fort at Port-Royal. As compared with Canada, Church and government were weak institutions, and the aristocracy insignificant. Outside Port-Royal, the settlers ran their civic affairs pretty much on their own, electing syndics from time to time to negotiate with a British commander, settling disputes through some form of informal arbitration (the details are obscure since the weakness of the State and the damage accompanying the deportation have deprived us of source materials). Becoming exasperated with what he saw as 'republican' tendencies among Acadian delegates who hesitated to take an oath of allegiance to His Britannic Majesty, Governor Edward Cornwallis lectured them sternly: 'It appears to me that you think yourselves independent of any government.'

It is easy to sentimentalize pre-deportation Acadia as a Garden of Eden, and a number of writers, starting with Henry Wadsworth Longfellow, have indeed portrayed it as a shining land of happy and virtuous rustics suddenly laid waste by an imperialist thunderbolt. Without reducing Acadian history to a simple stock plot, however, it is fair to regard the colony as something of a peasant paradise. Independent cultivators could live well, if simply, with no fear of famine or epidemic; no need to work for a master; and no significant exactions to support landlords, priests, or tax-collectors. Given the virtual absence of any other classes, to be an Acadian was to be a peasant in circumstances which, from the perspective of agrarian Europe, must have looked like peasant Valhalla.

After Acadia was formally ceded to Britain in 1713, France moved to occupy Cape Breton Island as a substitute foothold in this strategically and economically crucial area. Renaming the island Île Royale, the French quickly built it into a colony devoted to the cod fishery and maritime trade. While Mi'kmaq bands continued in possession of the largest part of the island, little fishing villages soon dotted the eastern shore and in their midst rose the massive bastions of Louisbourg. Louis XV's government poured millions into the capital city, making it one of colonial North America's few fully fortified towns, a major military and naval centre whose character was shaped by the growing imperial conflict pitting France against England. This warlike aspect did not prevent the fortress from falling to an invading force from New England in 1745. Diplomacy secured the return of Île Royale to France in 1749, but then, in 1758, the British once again laid siege to Louisbourg and captured the colony on their way to a larger victory in Canada. During the forty years it remained in French hands, Île Royale formed an exceptionally urbanized settlement; with 50 per cent of the colony's population, Louisbourg, in effect, was Île Royale.

The city dominated the colony and, in important ways, the military dominated the city. The basic layout of the town and its harbour was determined by military engineers. Building, repairing, and rebuilding the stone-covered earthworks around the perimeter, together with the various barracks and batteries, was a major local industry through most of French period. *Troupes de la marine*, who formed a much larger proportion of the population at Louisbourg than was the case even at Quebec or Montreal, supplied the bulk of the labour force; day after day, and for years on end, blue uniforms were drenched in sweat as soldiers strained to shovel earth and quarry rock. Their efforts entitled them to extra pay, but the money was channelled through their officers, and the latter found various pretexts to pocket the bulk of the men's earnings. Since the *troupes de la marine* at Louisbourg, unlike their Canadian counterparts, worked together in large construction gangs and lived together in a single barracks building, they were more likely to react as a group to festering grievances. Work stoppages and protests – the authorities called these 'riots' – erupted periodically. In the winter of 1744–5 long-standing tensions culminated in a full-scale mutiny, in the course of which the troops took over the town and extracted compensation at gunpoint from officers, government officials, and merchants who had cheated them in the past.

While war and preparations for war shaped Louisbourg's fortunes, Île Royale continued to draw its livelihood chiefly from the sea. Much more than Canada, this was a colony with a 'staple' economy; that is to say, it specialized in extracting and processing a single natural resource for sale overseas. Dried salt cod by the shipload left Île Royale, destined mainly for France and, increasingly over the years, for the French West Indies; its value in any given year dwarfed that of all the furs exported from the St Lawrence colony. Not only was the fishery productive and lucrative, it was to all intents and purposes the island's only industry and the sole employer of the great bulk of the civilian population. Agriculture, the main pursuit of other North American settler societies of the eighteenth century, was minimal, in part because of the rocky soil and forbidding climate of eastern Cape Breton. Yet even the fertile lands of Île St-Jean (Prince Edward Island), originally intended as a farming annex to Île Royale, were never successfully developed, and this agricultural failure simply underlines the overwhelming attractions of the fishery. The absence of a viable subsistence sector naturally affected Île Royale's economy, forcing it to import foodstuffs, along with all sorts of other supplies, but it also left no room for a self-sufficient peasantry or for an agrarian landlord class, and so the specialized fishing economy tended to structure colonial society in particular ways.

Catching, cleaning, and preserving codfish was strenuous and, given the unpredictability of the North Atlantic, dangerous work. It also demanded considerable skill, particularly when it came time to salt and dry the fish. By the eighteenth century, the 'habitant-pêcheurs' of Île Royale could draw upon customs and techniques developed by European-based crews which had been frequenting the area for a good two hundred years. Though French fishing ships still came to Cape Breton in the eighteenth century, colonial fishermen had the advantage of permanent shore facilities and the ability to fish almost year-round. They could also operate on a smaller scale. Typically an owner–operator with a wharf and adjacent shorefront would hire three or four men to help him: two would row out to sea for a day's fishing in a small boat ('chaloupe'), while the others worked as a shore crew. Schooners, larger vessels which could go farther afield and catch far more fish, became increasingly common over the years. But schooners were expensive, and small independent fishermen found it hard to compete with more highly capitalized entrepreneurs. Indeed, for a variety of reasons, fishing boats and facilities tended, towards mid-century, to come under the control of merchants, while more and more fishermen were reduced to the status of wage workers. This movement towards more capitalist arrangements paralleled similar developments in the Canadian fur trade at about the same time.

Merchants played an extremely important in role in this most mercantile of colonies. Even when they did not actually own and direct the fishing enterprises, traders were nevertheless intimately involved, supplying *habitant-pêcheurs* with salt, rum, and provisions on credit, and taking the salt cod in payment. Île Royale was utterly dependent on overseas commerce. France sold it salt, wine, cloth, and manufactured goods; Canada sent flour and ship's biscuit; from the West Indies came rum and sugar; and, finally, New England and Acadian Nova Scotia purveyed – more or less illegally – lumber, cattle, and agricultural livestock. Fish and more fish went abroad to pay for these imports. Possessing such a specialized commercial economy, Louisbourg was bound to be a busy seaport. Maritime traffic was even more intense than it might otherwise have been, because, in addition to relying heavily on imports and exports, Île Royale also served as an entrepôt port. Louisbourg was located at the centre of the French Atlantic, and so vessels from Canada, the West Indies, and France could all converge there, put their respective cargoes in warehouses, and procure what they needed from other points in the French empire, before returning home. Goods smuggled in from nearby New England only made Louisbourg that much more attractive as a port of call.

All this movement of commodities brought commissions and profits to the colonial merchants. Tidy fortunes were won by men such as Michel Daccarrette, who came to the colony as a humble Basque fisherman, but soon pursued entrepreneurial activities in fishing, shipbuilding, and over-

seas commerce. Comparatively numerous, but also confident and expansive, the traders of Louisbourg extended
their control into all aspects of the fishery. They also enjoyed considerable political influence over the colonial administration. Their prominence as an élite was almost unrivalled because in Île Royale, unlike Canada, the privileged
'estates' (clergy and nobility) were very weakly represented.
In all Louisbourg there was no proper parish church and no
parish clergy; instead, missionaries of the Récollet order
held Mass in the chapel of the King's Bastion. The Sisters of
the Congrégation de Notre-Dame operated a school for
girls, and the Récollets had one for boys, but otherwise the
Catholic Church was nowhere to be found. There were
some nobles, almost all of them military officers, but these
had only the shallowest roots in the colony. In the absence
of a viable agriculture, there were no real seigneuries and,
without seigneuries, there was no landed basis for a colonial
aristocracy.

Harvesting the resources of the continental shelf, trading
with the farthest corners of the Atlantic world, and preparing for the clash of overseas empires: these were the dominant activities in Île Royale. This eighteenth-century colony
turned its face to the sea as resolutely as Canada and Acadia
turned theirs towards the land. It reflected a certain aspect
of French society in the early modern period, that portion
dedicated to the pursuit of profit through the buying and
selling of commodities and labour. The divergent interests
of employers and workers, military and civilian, underlay
some of the serious social tensions in this version of European colonial society.

Canada's, of course, was a different sort of North American society, and inland from Canada proper lay the vast *pays
d'en haut*, where Natives and Europeans cohabited in a
unique way. This was not really a colonial society, but rather
Native-controlled land in which the French maintained an
important strategic and commercial presence. Down through
the Mississippi river system, they also maintained some tiny

outposts; far to the south, on the Gulf of Mexico, was Louisiana, yet another variety of colonial society, this one with affinities to the sugar islands of the West Indies. One way to visit these southern and western regions is in the company of Pierre-François-Xavier de Charlevoix, who wrote a book about his travels in 1721 from the St Lawrence settlements, through the *pays d'en haut*, and down the Mississippi to the port of New Orleans. Charlevoix was a French professor who had spent several years teaching at the college in Quebec; a Jesuit, but an eighteenth-century Jesuit, Charlevoix expressed the viewpoint less of a evangelizing fanatic than of an enlightened advocate of French empire.

The first stage of his canoe journey took him as far as 'the Narrows' between Lakes Erie and St Clair. This was Detroit, 'the finest part of all Canada,' according to Charlevoix: 'the river and lake abound in fish, the air is pure, and the climate temperate and extremely wholesome.' He hardly noticed the French fort, with its military garrison and its fur traders' depots; nor did he make much of the fledgling agricultural settlement, though by mid-century habitant farms lined the river, and Detroit was developing into a substantial French-Canadian colony. Instead, the traveller's attention was drawn to the Native villages which formed a more prominent feature of the local scene: one inhabited by Tionontate–Hurons, the amalgamated remnants of two Iroquoian nations destroyed in war eighty years earlier; another belonging to the Potawatomis; and a third made up of Ottawas. All these peoples grew corn, after the Iroquoian fashion, but the Potawatomis and Ottawa drew their subsistence more from fishing and hunting than from farming.

Geographically and politically, Detroit was in the midst of what historian Richard White calls the 'Middle Ground,' an area of complex interactions between Native people and Europeans. The Tionontate–Huron, Potawatomi, and Ottawa were here at least in part because of the French presence; they traded with the French and they acknowledged the king and his local commander as their 'father,' that is, as a dispenser of largesse, a coordinating leader in time of war, and a conciliator who settles disputes in peacetime. In no sense were they conquered nations. Canadians claimed the western interior for France, but, in their diplomatic and commercial dealings with the Natives, they had to acknowledge the basic independence of the latter and adapt to their ways. Natives, too, had to make compromises as, on the whole, they valued the goods supplied by Canadian traders and found security in the French-sponsored alliance system. Tensions were inevitable, for the interests of the various aboriginal nations frequently diverged from one another and from those of the French; moreover, the difference in cultures could lead to misunderstandings fraught with danger. If, for example, there was a glut on the European fur market and traders offered fewer knives for Native beaver skins, were the French trying to cheat their friends? Or if some personal quarrel ended with a Native killing a Frenchman, should this be considered a 'crime' that required a trial and punishment, or an injury that should be 'covered,' in the aboriginal fashion, by presents to the aggrieved family of the deceased? Leaders on both sides usually managed to find solutions to the various problems that arose, but the alliance required constant maintenance through presents, discussion, and negotiation.

While at Detroit, Father Charlevoix was privileged to witness a council of the three Native nations of Detroit and the French commandant, Monsieur de Tonti. Two items dominated the agenda: proposals to regulate the brandy trade, and a French effort to organize a concerted military campaign against the Outagamis (Foxes), an Algonquian nation which had fallen out with the allies several years earlier. For his European readers, Charlevoix sets the scene: 'naked savages' with strange hairstyles and 'not the least mark of distinction, nor any respect paid to any person whatsoever.' But these appearances of disorder are deceptive, he insists, for the meeting proceeded with the utmost dignity and decorum. 'It must be acknowledged, that proceedings are carried on in these assemblies with a wisdom and a coolness, and a knowledge of affairs, and I may add generally with a probity, which would have done honour to the areopagus of Athens, or to the senate of Rome, in the most glorious days of those republics.' The unnamed chief speaking on behalf of the Tionontate–Huron particularly impressed the classically trained Jesuit: 'His mien, the tone of his voice, and the manner of his delivery, though without any gestures or inflections of the body, appeared to me extremely noble and calculated to persuade.' The effect may have been 'charming,' but the substance of the speech constituted a rebuff to Tonti. Reproaching the French for making a separate peace with the Outagamis at an earlier stage of the war, the Tionontate–Huron and their allies declined to participate in any major offensive.

From Detroit, Charlevoix's route took him up Lake Huron to Michilimakinac, an important post at the entrance to Lake Michigan. His next stop was Green Bay, a rich region of fish, game, and wild rice where several Native nations had made their homes. There was a French fort and a mission establishment here, in the midst of villages of Menominee, Winnebago, Sauk, and many other peoples. Continuing south, Charlevoix made his way to a village of Miamis near the southern tip of Lake Michigan. Here the author observed a game of chance played with bundles of straws and pitting Miamis against a visiting group of Potawatomis. The Miamis, he observed, were also fond of lacrosse and played different versions of the game, depending on the number of players available. 'The players are divided into two companies who have each their own post, and the business is to toss the ball to that of the opposite party, without suffering it to fall to the ground or without touching it with the hand ... These Indians are so dexterous at catching the ball with their crosses, that sometimes a party lasts several days running.' Women, as well as men, played lacrosse.

Passing by easy portages into the Mississippi river system,

Charlevoix's party entered the land of the Illinois, a populous federation of four distinct nations, all of them relying for subsistence principally on the buffalo hunt and the cultivation of corn. The author considered them well disposed towards Christianity and reliable friends of the French. There was a Jesuit mission here, at Kaskaskia, and nearby a French military post, Fort Chartres. 'The French are now beginning to settle the country between this fort and the first mission. Four leagues farther and about a league from the river, is a large village inhabited by the French, who are almost all Canadians.' Nominally under the authority of Louisiana, the Illinois settlement emerged as a grain-growing colony shipping barges full of wheat flour down river to New Orleans. Slavery, though less prominent than in the lower Mississippi, was nevertheless more important here than in Canada. Out of a colonial population of 2,573 in 1752, Illinois numbered 890 black slaves and 147 Native slaves.

The opaque waters of the Mississippi concealed submerged branches that would quickly punch holes in a northern birchbark canoe, and so Charlevoix and his party embarked in hollowed-out cypress pirogues for the downstream voyage. Their destination was the lower reaches of the river, where the French were concentrating their colonizing efforts. Like Canada, Louisiana consisted of a small region fully occupied by the French, together with a vast hinterland inhabited by independent aboriginal nations who maintained some sort of connection with France. The whole colonial enterprise was at an early and somewhat uncertain stage when Charlevoix visited in 1721, and the infant plantations left him unimpressed. In New Orleans, still only a collection of rude huts, he found 'nothing very remarkable'; navigation on the lower Mississippi and the Gulf coast turned out to be treacherous in the extreme. Travelling as far as Biloxi, on the coast of what is now Mississippi, Charlevoix fell ill, though unlike hundreds of the early French settlers who succumbed to the deadly semi-tropical-disease climate of the region, he did recover his health. Biloxi and Mobile, the other French settlement on the Gulf of Mexico, drew their economic subsistence from the trade in deerskins with the up-country Choctaw Indians. Allies of the French, the Choctaws were locked in chronic conflict with the Chickasaws, the latter being trading partners with the English of South Carolina. English and French pressed on their respective allies and procured from them, not only huge supplies of deer hide, but also prisoners of war for enslavement.

Louisiana was notorious in France about the time of Charlevoix's visit, mainly because of the tremendous sums of money that had been poured into it, to no apparent good purpose, by John Law's Compagnie de l'Occident. Large numbers of convicts and *engagés* had been brought in from France and Germany, as well as some 2,000 African slaves, though half of all these newcomers died from disease. Population grew none the less, so that, by the end of the French regime, there were about 4,000 whites and 5,000 blacks in Louisiana. Natives, those living close to the colonial settlements together with the Indian nations of the up-country middle ground, remained much more numerous than blacks and whites combined. Charlevoix's disdain for the colony may have been connected to Louisiana's faltering economy, strikingly in contrast with the booming sugar economies of nearby St Domingue and other French islands of the West Indies. Louisiana did eventually develop a respectable trade with France, shipping out various products, including deerskins from the hinterland and plantation-grown tobacco and indigo.

Louisiana was an eighteenth-century colony and, like its contemporary, Île Royale, it had little of Canada's 'feudal' character. Avoiding seigneurial tenure, the government granted land directly to planters. Those able to command sufficient labour endeavoured to draw a profit from the soil by raising an export crop – usually tobacco or indigo – or corn or rice for sale on the colonial market. There were

habitant family farms, as well as plantations employing substantial slave and non-slave workforces. More common, however, were small-scale plantations on which the owner worked
side by side with two or three slaves or *engagés*. Opportunities in the agricultural sector were not unlimited, and so it
was common for rich planters to invest in trade as well as
agriculture, while the smaller settlers often departed on
expeditions into the interior to hunt deer or trade with the
Natives.

Over the years, slavery became an increasingly important
institution, drawing into its web hundreds of Indian people
and thousands of Africans. Black slavery never completely
overwhelmed Louisiana society, however; this was not the
West Indies, where a small minority of powerful planters
dominated an enslaved majority. Instead, poor whites remained numerous and, indeed, many of them – notably
soldiers and *engagés* – were at least temporarily unfree and
subject to much the same degrading regime as the enslaved
Africans. Plantation labour was often unbearably hard, and
the punishments meted out to slaves who attempted to
revolt or run away could be ghastly. On the other hand,
there was much more to slavery in French-regime Louisiana
than plantation field work. Many blacks were employed in
the towns as artisans and domestics; some even ranged the
interior as hunters, where, of necessity, they enjoyed considerable autonomy. Even agricultural field hands were usually
allowed some opportunity to grow crops for their own subsistence and profit. And, in spite of the best efforts of the
regime to pit Natives against Africans, many slaves did escape bondage and find freedom in an Indian village or in a
band of runaway black maroons. Manumissions also provided the colony with a substantial free black population. In
spite of its inherent brutality, then, the slave regime of
eighteenth-century Louisiana had a degree of fluidity
that contrasts with the more rigid racial slavery of the
nineteenth-century 'Old South.'

Daniel Usner, whose research has transformed our

understanding of the French colony on the Mississippi, emphasizes the 'cross-cultural interaction' which character- ized life in Louisiana. Aboriginals, Africans, and Europeans of all classes routinely came in close contact with one an- other. Sexual encounters and the resulting emergence of mixed-blood populations are only one aspect of this inter- mixing. The colony's 'foodways' also display evidence of cultural *métissage*. New Orleans consumed European wheat flour brought down from the Illinois, corn purchased from local Natives, rice which Africans had been instrumental in introducing to the delta wetlands, green vegetables grown by German settlers, okra favoured by black slaves, and bear grease (for cooking) purveyed by interior Indians. 'The origins of Louisiana's legendary creole cuisine,' states Usner, 'lie in the syncretic process of cultural change.' As with food, so with other aspects of culture: colonizers and colo- nized borrowed from each other, shaped and affected their respective ways of life, but without ever merging. Here, as in Canada, the ascendency of the French did not mean that subaltern peoples all assimilated to a single, European, norm. Instead, assimilation worked both ways to create one more distinctive North American colonial society.

Epilogue:

The Fall of New France

Built over the course of a century and a half, the French empire in North America suddenly collapsed between 1758 and 1760. The French had begun the Seven Years War (on this continent, 1754–60) with a string of victories, coupled with devastating frontier raids mounted by Natives and French Canadians. But eventually Britain, urged on by the beleaguered Thirteen Colonies, decided upon an all-out effort to crush French power in Canada. Though the conflict centred primarily on Europe (there it did actually last seven years, 1756–63) and involved clashes around the globe, Prime Minister William Pitt resolved to make the North American theatre a top priority. By the summer of 1758, some 42,000 British and colonial troops had been assembled, poised for the attack on New France. Just as significant, about one-quarter of the formidable British navy was deployed in the area, dominating the northwestern Atlantic so completely that supplies and reinforcements from France were effectively cut off. France and England had been squabbling in North America inconclusively for six decades, but now, quite suddenly, the balance of forces shifted dramatically against the French and, for the first time, the British could realistically aim, not simply at territorial gains and strategic advantages, but at total victory.

The naval blockade strangling trade into the St Lawrence was devastating in its effects on both Canada and the *pays d'en haut.* In the Laurentian colony, its effects combined with an unfortunate series of short harvests to produce a shortage of almost all vital commodities, above all, food. At the same time, an unprecedented military build-up and the voracious appetite for supplies that it accompanied placed impossible demands on colonial supplies. Urban civilians were particularly hard hit and, in the winter of 1758–9 starvation became a serious threat. In Quebec City, it was said, 'workers and artisans, ravaged by hunger, can no longer work; they are so weak they can hardly stand up.' In an effort to relieve the cities and ensure supplies to the military, squadrons of soldiers were sent into the countryside to requisition grain at the point of a gun. Meanwhile, in the *pays d'en haut*, post commanders lacked the gifts and trade goods needed to play the role of a proper 'father.' Moreover, the French, under the pressures of intensifying war, had been taking a high-handed approach with the Indian nations of the Great Lakes and the Ohio country, effectively abandoning the cultural compromises underpinning the 'middle ground,' and alienating their allies. Thus, when the British appeared on the horizon with substantial forces, most Native groups made peace with the invaders, in part in order to rid the country of the now hated French. These defections opened the way to the British, who soon captured Detroit and the other western posts.

Meanwhile, Canada was under attack by two major armies of invasion, one of them making its laborious way up the heavily defended corridor leading north via Lake Champlain to Montreal, the other taking a seaborne route by way of the Gulf of St Lawrence. This latter, amphibious, assault entailed a costly but successful siege of Louisbourg in 1758, followed by the siege of the hitherto impregnable defences of Quebec. Week after week in the summer of 1759, British batteries bombarded the capital without mercy, while raiding parties burned villages all up and down the St Lawrence in defiance of then current rules of civilized warfare. Finally, a decisive engagement on the Plains of Abraham delivered Quebec to the English. This battle, so widely known today because of its dramatic qualities, was really only one episode in a much larger campaign. Historians have pointed out that it was, in fact, a very near thing, which, with a little luck on their side, the French might well have won. But even so, would a different outcome on the Plains of Abraham have kept Canada French? Not likely. The British investment in the reduction of New France was simply overwhelming. Not one, but three armies were pressing into the colony, from the west and the south, as well as the east, and in the summer of 1760 they all bore down on the last French stronghold of Montreal. Its fate more or less sealed two years earlier, Canada was, on 9 September, finally surrendered to the invaders.

England was definitely on a winning streak in the later part of the Seven Years War. Its European ally, Prussia, emerged victorious in central Europe, and Britain itself captured French possessions around the world: slaving stations on the coast of Africa, colonial establishments in India, and precious sugar islands in the West Indies. Then Spain entered the war on France's side, and the English promptly took Havana and Manila. In the complicated diplomatic arrangements which concluded the war (1763), Britain acquired title – strictly within the realm of European imperial pretensions, of course – to most of North America. France retained fishing rights on the coast of Newfoundland, but Île Royale was annexed to Nova Scotia, and Canada was recognized as a British province. Louisiana, which had been largely untouched by the fighting, was divided: the western part, including New Orleans, went to Spain, while Britain acquired the eastern part along with formerly Spanish Florida.

And where are the people of New France in this geopolitical story of conquest and defeat? Did the social configurations sketched out in earlier sections of this book play any part in provoking war? Nineteenth-century historians sometimes suggested that a fight to the finish between the French and the English in North America was somehow the product of essential differences in the two nationalities which led to the formation of fundamentally incompatible colonial societies, and vestiges of that view can still be found in modern interpretations. Equally influential – and just as misleading, in my opinion – is the notion that New France was doomed to be a loser in the inevitable struggle because of some sort of basic fatal flaw.

Certainly there were important differences distinguishing the French and English colonial societies in North America: differences in language, religion, political institutions, and relations between Natives and European colonists. But there was also great diversity within each of the two camps. Within the broadly delineated New France of the eighteenth century could be found the comparatively Europeanized society of Canada, with its military aristocracy; its seigneurial agrarian life; and its towns, with their diverse assortment of merchants, artisans, priests, nuns, soldiers, and officials. Île Royale, on the other hand, displayed a much more capitalist character, with fishing and trading to the fore and little trace of any feudal elements, whereas Acadia had been dominated by its free peasantry. Slavery and plantation agriculture were prominent features of life in Louisiana. And in the backcountry claimed by Louisiana, as well as Canada's *pays d'en haut*, various aboriginal modes of existence prevailed, and the handful of French who frequented these regions had to adapt to that reality. French North America, like English North America, was not a homogeneous whole. In searching out the causes of all-out war, one might just as well point to affinities linking neighbouring sections of the rival empires – Louisiana and South Carolina, Canada and New York, Île Royale and Massachusetts – as attempt to find some essential cultural dichotomy.

The fact is that, through most of the colonial period, New France and English America were at peace, and when they did come to blows, it was seldom over genuinely colonial issues. Aboriginal nations such as the Mi'kmaq had basic and enduring motives for hostility towards the colonizing powers, and since the English usually posed a greater threat, they often ended up allying themselves with the French. But French Canadians had little cause, obedience to their monarch apart, for fighting New Englanders. There was always a certain amount of border skirmishing in peripheral regions of uncertain ownership, such as Newfoundland and Hudson Bay, but, by and large, the two nations colonized separate regions and had few points of friction. Historians used to believe that competition over the western fur-trade drove the English and French colonizers into mortal combat, but recent research indicates that international fur trade rivalries were more a result than a cause of international hostilities; the two powers used the fur trade in an attempt to attract Native nations into their respective commercial-diplomatic orbits. Indeed, it seems quite likely that, if left to their own devices, French Canadians and Anglo-Americans would have shared the continent just as the Spanish and Portuguese shared South America, not always in peace perhaps, but without harbouring plans to destroy each other's settlements utterly.

In colonial North America, war – that is, war between English and French, though not war between colonizers and Natives – was largely a European import. Canada went to war because France went to war. Men from the Iroquoian communities of the St Lawrence, along with *troupes de la marine* and French-Canadian militia, as well as allied Natives from the *pays d'en haut*, relied mainly on guerrilla raids to harass the designated enemy to the south. As long as war was conducted mainly by North Americans, New France more than held its own; even though it was vastly outnumbered by the Anglo-Americans, authoritarian French Canada was organized for war and, more important, it could rely on Native support. Thus, the idea that defects in French colonial society preordained the defeat of 1760 are hard to credit, since Canada's military record suggests strength rather than weakness through most of the period. In a sense, that very strength itself led to the downfall, in that early French successes in the Seven Years War helped to galvanize England and British North America into an extraordinary mobilization of forces. What sealed the doom of New France was the sudden Europeanization of the conflict in 1758. When Britain poured men, ships, and equipment into the fray, the mode of fighting changed abruptly, as did the balance of forces, and Canada's brand of frontier raiding was now of little account. In sum, New France's involvement in major war, and also its ultimate defeat, were mainly the result of European intervention; they were not determined by the shape of its colonial society.

And what of the consequences of the Conquest? Generations of Canadians, English- as well as French-speaking, have come to view this event as the central cataclysm in their country's history, a humiliating defeat which lies at the root of Quebec nationalism, and a heavy blow to the social development of French Canada which left it backward and impoverished for centuries to come. Of course, the Conquest did ultimately have far-reaching effects for Canada; without it there would never have been an English Canada, nor would there have been a binational federal state. But was French Canada humiliated by the Conquest and did it then enter a period of social disarray?

That is certainly not the way it appeared to most contemporaries in the 1760s. Then it seemed clear that England had beaten France in a war and had taken Canada as its prize. French Canadians had no reason to feel like a defeated and humbled people, and there is little indication that they did feel that way in the decades following the Conquest. There may have been some apprehension that property would be threatened, that the Catholic religion would be persecuted, or even that residents would be deported as the Acadians and the people of Île Royale had been only a few years earlier. These concerns proved groundless, however, for, with the war now at an end, Britain had no need and no desire to depopulate the colony. There were, indeed, some troublesome issues surrounding the legal system, the status of the Church, and the admission of French Canadians to public office. Moreover, some residents – mostly government officials, merchants, and military officers – quit the colony as soon as it passed into Britain's empire, though it is an exaggeration to refer to this exodus as a social 'decapitation,' particularly when many of the emigrants were metropolitan French who would likely have left Canada even if it had remained under the rule of France. As a colony, New France had always been dominated by European intendants, bishops, and, to a large extent, judges and merchants. After 1760 it would be ruled by a different set of outsiders who happened to be British. This did not seem remarkable to most contemporaries, for nationalism – the belief that government and governed should have the same ethnic and linguistic identity – was not then a powerful force anywhere in the world.

The idea that French Canada was a conquered nation rather than a ceded colony was the product of a very different epoch, one that began almost a century after the conclusion of the Seven Years War. Between the Conquest and the emergence of the Myth of the Conquest stretched a long and eventful period of history filled with momentous developments in Canada and around the Atlantic world. The American Revolution, the Haitian Revolution, and the Latin American wars of independence brought European imperial rule to an end throughout most of the western hemisphere. With the French Revolution and the wars of Napoleon, *anciens régimes* crumbled and the 'principle of nationality' gained adherents across Europe. French Canada felt the force of these global developments. One result was the nationalist-democratic Rebellion of 1837–8, a revolt against British rule inspired by a republican vision of national independence (not, as some have suggested, by any sort of desire to return to Bourbon rule). Only after the defeat of this insurrection, and after the predominantly

French portion of Canada (Lower Canada) had been yoked politically to English-speaking parts of British North America, did chastened and more conservative elements of the French-Canadian élite begin to speak longingly of the glories of New France. Along with the idealization of the supposedly conservative and Catholic French régime went a view of French–English conflict as inveterate, enduring, and unchanging. This idea that 'the English' were the enemy and that the Conquest had been a social disaster that ruined French Canada's development began to enjoy wide appeal in the second half of the nineteenth century; this was when the French were losing political influence to a rapidly expanding English Canada, and when ordinary French Canadians found their lives disrupted by a capitalism that seemed to speak only English and to benefit only anglophones. The Myth of the Conquest, the belief that the cession constituted an epoch-making tragedy with social as well as political dimensions, was a product of French Canada's social stresses in the 1860s, not the 1760s. And, as the political economy of Canadian capitalism continued to develop to the disadvantage of French Quebec, the Myth of the Conquest continued to hold sway throughout the twentieth century.

Canada in the immediate wake of the Conquest was certainly a traumatized society, but the trauma it suffered had been caused much more by the war itself than by the cession to Britain. Especially in Quebec City and its region, the physical destruction had been immense, not to mention the economic dislocation occasioned by the blockade and famine. To make matters worse, the French government's partial renunciation of its debts wrecked many colonial fortunes. Rebuilding took years. But the Conquest as such – the transfer of New France from one empire to another – struck at French-Canadian society only in limited and selective ways.

For most people, and in most aspects of existence, the advent of British rule made little difference. The habitants – which is to say, the great majority of French Canadians –

continued their agrarian way of life, colonizing ever-expanding territories on the edges of the St Lawrence valley. Basic family self-sufficiency remained central, but increasingly habitants lucky enough to possess prime wheat-growing lands grew substantial surpluses for sale overseas. Access to British imperial market helped stimulate this development, but the trend towards export agriculture had been set long before the Conquest. Tithes and seigneurial exactions continued more or less as before, though some of the seigneurs were now English merchants and officers who had purchased seigneuries from emigrating French seigneurs. Over the decades, seigneurial rents tended to bear down more heavily on the peasantry as land became more scarce and agriculture more lucrative, but, again, the tendency under the British regime was the culmination of developments begun under the French regime; the Conquest was largely incidental.

At the top levels of French-Canadian society, the change in imperial masters posed serious problems. The clergy were no longer subsidized, nor were they integrated into the State, now officially Protestant. However, the Catholic Church weathered the storm quite nicely, quietly developing a working relationship with a succession of British governors and discovering, for the rest, the benefits of ecclesiastical independence beyond the reach of their Most Catholic Majesties of France. The *noblesse* was damaged badly by the elimination of the colonial military force and of the officers' careers it had come to depend on. The rising value of seigneurial incomes helped to cushion the blow, but nobles could no longer look to government for preferment as they had in the past. Canadian merchants were also damaged by the Conquest. Traders from Britain and the Thirteen Colonies swarmed into the St Lawrence valley hard on the heels of the conquering armies, bringing low-priced merchandise that undercut resident merchants. Business connections with Britain and contacts with the occupying army were at a premium now that Canada's commerce had to be redirected into a different imperial system, and so French-Canadian importers and exporters were immediately placed at a disadvantage. The fur traders of Montreal held out for a time, but, within twenty years, anglophone capitalists dominated even that branch of commerce.

Was the Conquest good or bad for women? In most essential respects, it seems to have left power relations between the sexes unchanged. French-Canadian civil law, including the rules defining marital property rights and inheritance, remained in place after an initial period of uncertainty following the cession. Visitors from overseas – British now, rather than French – still remarked on the independent and domineering character of the Canadian ladies. There were certainly major realignments of gender ideology in the nineteenth century, as public life was, with increasing insistence, declared off limits to women. This occurred long after the Conquest, however, and the change clearly mirrored widespread international trends, discernible in France itself, as well as in England and English-speaking North America.

The Iroquois, Huron, and other Natives resident in the St Lawrence colony certainly suffered as a result of the Conquest; or, to put it more accurately, the conclusion of French–English conflict reduced the Natives' value as military auxiliaries and gave them less bargaining power and room to manoeuvre. Officials under the British regime wished to retain the allegiance of the local aboriginal population, particularly as war once again loomed: against the United States and France. After the 1820s, peace seemed more assured and Iroquois assistance less necessary, and subsidies meant to reward allegiance were phased out. Encroachment on their land base at Kahnawaké and Oka undermined the Natives' agrarian economy, just at a time when government tribute was disappearing. Many men sought external income working in the Northwest fur trade and the forest industry, but impoverishment was the fate of these Native communities in the post-Conquest era.

In the *pays d'en haut*, war's end brought a painful transition as options suddenly closed down for the aboriginal nations of the west. The Seven Years War had kept American settlers and land speculators at bay, but soon they were pouring over the Appalachians in spite of Britain's efforts to reserve the territory to Amerindians. Moreover, the British military, after dislodging the French from Detroit and other posts in the region, settled in as an army of occupation in spite of Native protests. They also cut off 'presents,' the tribute previously offered as a token of alliance. The overall refusal of the British to play the role of a good alliance 'father' provoked the reconstitution of an anti-British alliance of many western tribes which, under Pontiac's leadership, came close to driving the British out of the region. One enduring legacy of the period of French ascendancy in the *pays d'en haut* was the tradition of Pan-Indian alliances. Creating unity out of these culturally diverse and politically fragmented groups was exceedingly difficult, but, from Pontiac's time until the early nineteenth century, a series of concerted efforts did help slow the Anglo-American onslaught. The fact that the British, now embroiled in conflict with their colonists, were prevailed upon to take up aspects of Onontio's role was certainly a factor, but the impulse to resist came largely from the Natives themselves.

New France did indeed disappear, both in its narrow 'Canadian' sense and in its wider, continental meaning, encompassing the *pays d'en haut* and the scattered enclaves of French settlement. After the Conquest, the Maritime region took on a distinctly British character. The residents of Île Royale were all deported, though with less brutality than the Acadian removal a few years earlier. Soon Yankee settlers from New England spread through the region, followed by British immigrants and Loyalist refugees; when Acadians began to straggle back years later, they found themselves geographically, culturally, and politically marginalized. In Louisiana, the French and African elements of colonial society, along with the institution of slavery, persisted under Spain's rule. The arrival of Acadian refugees to colonize the bayous of the lower Mississippi only reinforced the French quality of the colony. Under Napoleon, France repossessed Louisiana, then promptly sold it to the young American republic. Society was thoroughly Americanized in the nineteenth century, though French and Creole ways subsisted as picturesque folkloric vestiges.

If we were to seek for the legacy of New France, we might find it, at the most superficial level, in the French place-names – Coeur d'Alene, Terre Haute, Port Mouton – strewn across North America and regularly mispronounced by the current inhabitants. It might also be found in the various pockets in Canada and the United States where French is still spoken. More significantly, of course, the Canadian settlement along the banks of the St Lawrence established frameworks – language, customs, law – for the development of modern Quebec (not that one would wish to portray French Quebec as a mere survival left over from the French regime; contemporary Quebec has been shaped by its colonial past no more and no less than Connecticut or Ontario). There is a third aspect to the legacy of New France, broader in scope and more profound in its implications than the other two mentioned so far: that is its role as a critical part of the colonial history of North America generally.

The thrust of this book has been to present the people of New France as participants in a momentous and multidimensional process of colonization, one in which mere 'Frenchness' is only part of the story. In the seventeenth and eighteenth centuries, Catholic immigrants from France, working often in close relations with Natives, blacks, and Protestants, reconstituted a version of European society on the banks of the St Lawrence. The settler society of 'Canada' spawned smaller French colonies, none of them homogeneously French, in the Great Lakes, the Mississippi, and the Maritimes. Through the process of expansion, the French collided with, traded with, fought, wooed, and allied themselves with dozens of aboriginal peoples, from the Arctic to the Gulf of Mexico. This was one element, though a crucially important one, of the broad process of colonization which also involved other Natives of North America, as well as English, Spanish, and Dutch settlers, and enslaved Africans. In that it constituted, not simply a community of transplanted Europeans, but a complicated pattern of Native–European interaction over a vast terrain, New France shaped the destinies of a continent.

Select Bibliography

General Works

Charlevoix, Pierre de. *Journal of a Voyage to North-America Under-taken by Order of the French King*, 2 vols. London: R. and J. Dodsley 1761

Dechêne, Louise. *Habitants and Merchants in Seventeenth-Century Montreal*, trans. L. Vardi. Montreal: McGill–Queen's University Press 1992

Eccles, W.J. *France in America*. Markham, Ont.: Fitzhenry & Whiteside 1990

Harris, R. Cole, ed. *Historical Atlas of Canada*, Vol. 1: *From the Beginning to 1800*. Toronto: University of Toronto Press 1986

Kalm, Peter. *Peter Kalm's Travels in North America*, trans. Adolph Benson. New York: Dover 1937

Miquelon, Dale. *New France, 1701–1744: 'A Supplement to Europe.'* Toronto: McClelland & Stewart 1987

Trudel, Marcel. *Introduction to New France*. Toronto: Holt, Rinehart & Winston 1968

Chapter 1 Population

Charbonneau, Hubert. *The First French Canadians: Pioneers in the St. Lawrence Valley*. Newark, N.J.: University of Delaware Press 1993

– *Vie et mort de nos ancêtres. Etude démographique*. Montreal: Les Presses de l'Université de Montréal 1975

Gauvreau, Danielle. *Québec, une ville et sa population au temps de la Nouvelle-France*. Sillery: Les Presses de l'Université du Québec 1991

Landry, Yves. *Orphelines en France, pionnières au Canada: Les filles du roi au XVIIe siècle*. Montreal: Léméac 1992

Landry, Yves, and Rénald Lessard. 'Les Causes de décès aux XVIIe et XVIIIe siècles d'après les registres paroissiaux québécois.' *Revue d'histoire de l'Amérique française* 48 (1995): 509–26

Moogk, Peter N. 'Reluctant Exiles: Emigrants from France in Canada before 1760.' *William and Mary Quarterly*, 3rd ser., 46 (1989): 463–505

Chapter 2   Life on the Land

Dechêne, Louise. *Le Partage des substistences au Canada sous le régime français*. Montreal: Boréal 1994

Desbarats, Catherine. 'Agriculture within the Seigneurial Regime of Eighteenth-Century Canada: Some Thoughts on the Recent Literature.' *Canadian Historical Review* 73 (March 1992): 1–29

Greer, Allan. *Peasant, Lord and Merchant: Rural Society in Three Quebec Parishes, 1740–1840*. Toronto: University of Toronto Press 1985

Harris, R.C. *The Seigneurial System in Early Canada: A Geographical Study*. Madison: University of Wisconsin Press 1966

Lavallée, Louis. *La Prairie en Nouvelle-France, 1647–1760: Étude d'histoire sociale*. Montreal: McGill–Queen's University Press 1992

Chapter 3   The Urban Landscape

Bosher, J.F. *The Canada Merchants, 1713–1763*. New York: Oxford University Press 1987

Eccles, W.J. 'The Social, Economic, and Political Significance of the Military Establishment in New France.' *Canadian Historical Review* 52 (March 1971): 1–22

Gadoury, Lorraine. *La Noblesse de Nouvelle-France: Familles et alliances.* Montreal: Hurtubise HMH 1991

Lachance, André. *La Vie urbaine en Nouvelle-France.* Montreal: Boréal 1987

Miquelon, Dale. 'Havy and Lefebvre of Quebec: A Case Study of Metropolitan Participation in Canadian Trade, 1730–60.' *Canadian Historical Review* 56 (1975): 1–24

Moogk, Peter. 'Apprenticeship Indentures: A Key to Artisan Life in New France.' Canadian Historical Association, *Historical Papers,* 1971, 65–83

Chapter 4 Women of New France

Bégon, Elisabeth. *Lettres au cher fils. Correspondance d'Elisabeth Bégon avec son gendre (1748–1753).* Montréal: Hurtubise HMH 1972

Choquette, Leslie. '"Ces Amazones du Grand Dieu": Women and Mission in Seventeenth-Century Canada.' *French Historical Studies* 17 (Spring 1992): 627–55

Cliche, Marie-Aimée. *Les Pratiques de dévotion en Nouvelle-France: Comportements populaires et encadrement ecclésial dans le gouvernement de Québec.* Quebec: Les Presses de l'Université Laval 1988

Gauvreau, Danielle. *Québec, une ville et sa population au temps de la Nouvelle-France.* Sillery: Les Presses de l'Université du Québec 1991

Noel, Jan. 'New France: Les femmes favorisées.' In *Rethinking Canada: The Promise of Women's History,* ed. V. Strong-Boag and A. Fellman, 23–44. Toronto: Copp Clark 1986

Rapley, Elizabeth. *The Dévotes: Women and Church in Seventeenth-Century France.* Montreal: McGill–Queen's University Press 1990

Spittal, W.G., ed. *Iroquois Women: An Anthology.* Ohoweken, Ont.: Iroqrafts 1990

Ulrich, Laurel Thatcher. *Good Wives: Image and Reality in the Lives of Women in Northern New England, 1650–1750.* New York: Knopf 1982

Chapter 5   French and Others

Axtell, James. *The Invasion Within: The Contest of Cultures in Colonial North America.* New York: Oxford University Press 1985

Bédard, Marc-André. *Les Protestants en Nouvelle-France.* Quebec: Société historique de Québec 1978

Delâge, Denys. *Bitter Feast: Amerindians and Europeans in Northeast North America, 1600–64.* Vancouver: UBC Press 1993

Demos, John. *The Unredeemed Captive: A Family Story from Early America.* New York: Norton 1994

Jetten, Marc. *Enclaves amérindiennes: Les 'Réductions' du Canada, 1637–1701.* Sillery: Septentrion 1994

Richter, Daniel K. *The Ordeal of the Longhouse: The Peoples of the Iroquois League in the Era of European Colonization.* Chapel Hill: University of North Carolina Press 1992

Snow, Dean. *The Iroquois.* Oxford: Blackwell 1994

Trigger, Bruce. *Natives and Newcomers: Canada's 'Heroic Age' Reconsidered.* Montreal: McGill–Queen's University Press 1985

Trudel, Marcel. *L'Esclavage au Canada français: Histoire et conditions de l'esclavage.* Quebec: Les Presses de l'Université Laval 1960

Chapter 6   Beyond Canada

Bailey, A.G. *The Conflict of European and Eastern Algonkian Cultures, 1504–1700.* Toronto: University of Toronto Press 1969

Clark, Andrew H. *Acadia: The Geography of Early Nova Scotia to 1760.* Madison: University of Wisconsin Press 1968

Dièreville, Sieur de. *Relation of a Voyage to Port Royal in Acadia or New France.* Ed. J.C. Webster. Toronto: Champlain Society 1933

Griffiths, Naomi. *The Contexts of Acadian History, 1686–1784.* Montreal: McGill–Queen's University Press 1992

Krause, Eric, Carol Corbin, and William O'Shea, eds. *Aspects of Louisbourg.* Sydney: University College of Cape Breton 1995

Moore, Christopher. *Louisbourg Portraits: Life in an Eighteenth-Century Garrison Town.* Toronto: Macmillan 1982

Usner, Daniel H. *Indians, Settlers, & Slaves in a Frontier Exchange Economy: The Lower Mississippi Valley before 1783*. Chapel Hill: University of North Carolina Press 1992

White, Richard. *The Middle Ground: Indians, Empires and Republics in the Great Lakes Region, 1650–1815*. New York: Cambridge University Press 1991

Epilogue The Fall of New France

Cook, Ramsay. *The Maple Leaf Forever: Essays on Nationalism and Politics in Canada*. Toronto: Macmillan 1971

Frégault, Guy. *Canada: the War of the Conquest*. Trans. M. Cameron. Toronto: Oxford University Press 1969

Miquelon, Dale, ed. *Society and Conquest: The Debate on the Bourgeoisie and Social Change in French Canada, 1700–1850*. Toronto: Copp Clark 1977

Stanley, G.F.G. *New France: The Last Phase, 1744–1760*. Toronto: McClelland & Stewart 1968

Index

THEMES IN CANADIAN SOCIAL HISTORY

Editors: Craig Heron and Franca Iacovetta